Wasp

Animal
Series editor: Jonathan Burt

Wasp

Richard Jones

REAKTION BOOKS

Published by
REAKTION BOOKS LTD
Unit 32, Waterside
44–48 Wharf Road
London N1 7UX, UK
www.reaktionbooks.co.uk

First published 2019
Copyright © Richard Jones 2019

Printed and bound in China by 1010 International Ltd

A catalogue record for this book is available from the British Library

ISBN 978 1 78914 161 0

Contents

Introduction

Fear and fascination in equal measure set wasps apart from other insects. The frisson of danger evoked by the threat of a painful sting has given them an undeserved reputation for aggressiveness bordering on vindictive spite. Though arguably they really are just a specialized group of wasps, bees have gone on to be lauded by humans, but wasps are vilified. Unlike honeybees (industrious), and bumblebees (cuddly), wasps are viewed by humans with the same lack of empathy they feel for spiders and scorpions.

The relatively large size of wasps, their bright colours and communal nesting make them far more visible than many insects, and their unwanted attentions at the picnic table bring them into closer human contact than many would prefer. This mistrust is deep-seated in a human history that has easily awarded value (commercial and spiritual) to bees but which has failed to recognize any worth in wasps, except in echoing their danger. Black-and-yellow rugby shirts warn opponents that the Coventry team is not to be messed with. Such is the strength of the black-and-yellow danger signal that this is now the default warning in industrial hazard zones, on road signs, to mark broken steps awaiting repair, danger from sharp edges, mind the barrier, keep out, leave it alone, don't touch.

Back in the natural world, bees and wasps are constantly mixed up and muddled, to the great confusion of journalists on tight schedules. Widespread mimicry by harmless flies, moths and beetles utilizes this muddle, which extends beyond frustrated picture editors to potential animal predators less than enthusiastic about tackling a prey item that might fight back with a painful sting.

The black-and-yellow livery of wasps makes them attractive and exciting, and their distinctive forms have been depicted in art and literature down the years. No still-life painting is complete without the embellishment of insects as decorative baubles, and the strong colours of wasps make them perfect touches. From the juror chorus in Aristophanes' play *The Wasps* to a mad reinterpretation of an Agatha Christie novel in a *Doctor Who* episode, wasps make regular appearances across all media down the ages because they are distinctive, recognizable and well known. Except they are not as well known as their stereotype would have us believe.

Despite their iconic form and characteristic colours, wasps are still surrounded by myth and misunderstanding. Wasp 'facts' as they might be imagined by the vast majority of the populace are,

Queen wasps depicted with a bumblebee, all going about their charming routine lives. Calling the queen wasp 'a winter survivor and foundress of a new colony' indicates a certain respect for an oft-maligned insect. From the anonymously published *Episodes of Insect Life* (1850).

in fact, anything but – they are fanciful folklore little changed since before the Dark Ages. Aristotle (384–322 BC) had a fine mind and is rightly celebrated as a key natural philosopher (as near to a scientist as it was then possible to be), but he was foremost a philosopher on a general scale, not an expert biologist or entomologist by today's standards, and much of what he thought about the natural world is now known to be wildly incorrect. Yet much of modern society's view of wasps is still informed by the thinking of his time, and this information is now 2,000 years out of date. Worse, wasp knowledge is often based on cartoon-like stereotypes bordering on sad parody. Is it any wonder that scare stories erupt in the tabloid press late every summer when, surprise surprise, there seem to be lots of wasps about? To top it all the long-awaited Asian hornet, a pest of mind-boggling proportions to tabloid editors, has just been found in the UK. Disaster looms. Maybe.

Wasps have long fascinated biologists for their complex nesting and colony behaviour. A caste system based on sterile worker females and a ruling queen, with intermittent indolent males, is controlled by a strange genetic process based on chromosome number, chemical pheromone signals and larval nutrition. Their powerful carnivorous nature makes them important predators of other insects, giving them a major role in the centre of many food webs. Even the venom, the source of that sharp, painful, stinging defence that so defines wasps, is a marvellous cocktail mix of bioactive chemicals just waiting to be exploited by the pharmaceutical industry.

Wasps are more than the stinger in the tip of the tail. They are worthy of greater understanding and appreciation. Where now they are often regarded as awful, wasps should really be regarded as awesome.

1 A Sting in the Tale

If only one thing is known about wasps, it is that they sting. The pain may vary from a puzzling pinprick to a howl-inducing hot dagger stab and it may fade in moments or remain a flesh-numbing throb that aches for days. A sting, though, is usually just a minor inconvenience – a personal measure of the sensitivity of human skin. The welt, if one appears, is a trivial wound, but the power of the wasp's venom, and the seeming tenacity of their attacks, marks out these otherwise insignificant creatures as dangerous and vengeful. However, wasps are less dangerous than honeybees; and hornets (an epithet reserved for the largest of wasps) are unfairly labelled with a curmudgeonly disposition they do not possess. The sting in the tail of a wasp has elevated what is in effect a tiny insect into a monster of phantasmagorical proportions. Yet, as with so many human anxieties, this is a fear based on ignorance – in reality there is no such thing as monsters.

The sting did get wasps noticed, though, and our ancestors soon gave these specks of painful animosity a name. The simple common English name 'wasp' is clearly derived from the Latin *vespa*, a term still used in the scientific literature as the generic name for hornets. Likely their colloquial nickname 'jasper' also came from here. This root is expanded into myriad similar names in other European languages – *Wespe* in German, *wesp* in Dutch, *hveps* in Danish, *veps* in Norwegian, *avispa* in Spanish and

Beautiful hand-painted wasps from *The Natural History of British Insects* (1792–1813) by esteemed British naturalist Edward Donovan. Yet still bee muddles occur: his caption states, 'they collect the juices of fruits, insects, &c. and make honey, but it is inferior to that of bees.'

guêpe (formerly *guespe*) in French. In early English writings it was sometimes distorted to wops or wapse – perhaps illiterate mis-renderings or childish jumblings.

The trouble is that our ancestors were not expert insect taxonomists and there has been a constant muddle over any small creature that stings, bites or just buzzes around looking a bit menacing. The modern word hornet comes from Old English *hyrnet* (also *harnette, hyrnitu, hyrnet*), and is thought to be somehow linked with horn, but whether this was for its tough orange-brown carapace or a loud buzzing vuvuzela sound is uncertain. Perhaps it rests on the hornet's reputation for aggression, as in the splendid archaic phrase 'horn-mad' – enraged, like an angry horned bull. In Dutch *horzel* can mean hornet, but it is also used for horse flies (large blood-suckers in the fly family Tabanidae) – unpleasant and off-putting, maybe, but a completely different group of insects. The Welsh for wasp is variously given as *kakkyman, cacynen, ngha-cynen* alongside various other dialectical variants, and also *gwenyn meirch*, which is literally 'horse bee'. Common or vernacular names are often fraught with difficulty.

The earliest depictions of wasps are in ancient Egyptian hiero-glyphs from 5,000 years ago,[1] but any entomologist will look askance at these crude stone engravings and wonder whether the designs are wasp, hornet or (most likely) honeybee – a confusion that still reigns today. The stylized insect carvings are not helped by the frequent depiction of only four legs – hardly an endorse-ment of the ancient artist's credibility when it comes to anatomical accuracy. Aristotle had a reasonable knowledge of some wasps, and he makes many astute observations. He knew there was a mother (or 'leader') wasp in the nest (just like in honeybee hives), larger and gentler than the run-of-the-mill workers; he knew that these could hibernate over winter 'lurking in holes', but he seemed uncertain whether they could sting (they can). But 2,000 years of

From an intricately carved ancient Egyptian stone facia, a hiero-glyphic winged insect – but whether wasp or honeybee is still open to debate; wing and leg number do not help in the identification.

linguistic and scientific reinterpretation leaves many shadows and it is often unclear what types of insect he and his contemporaries were really describing in their various texts. He used many names like *Sphex*, *Crabro* (supposedly after the town Crabra in Tusculanum where they were abundant), *Agrion* and *Anthrene* (so called because the sting raised a carbuncle or anthrar, a variant of anthrax).[2] Some of these names are today reused for completely different organisms – *Sphex* and *Crabro* are now genera of small solitary wasps, but *Agrion* refers to a group of delicate (and non-stinging) dragonflies. *Anthrenus* is now the carpet beetle of domestic pest fame; although from the same root the similar *Andrena* is used for a broad group of small solitary bees – though whether their stings are powerful enough to raise a carbuncle in the flesh is very doubtful.

This confusion is not helped by the fact that the concept of wasp still has a sometimes vague and nebulous fluidity. Just like the 'fly' in butterfly and dragonfly, which are patently not flies, the title 'wasp' is applied almost haphazardly to a whole host of different creatures. Despite advances in scientific understanding, modern entomologists have not always assisted. To start, then, it is important to work out exactly what we mean by 'wasp'.

WHAT MAKES A WASP?

Broadly speaking, wasps belong to the hyperdiverse insect order Hymenoptera, from the Greek   , *humeno pteros*, meaning 'membrane-winged'. Wasps have four clear membranous wings, unadorned by the colourful scales of butterflies and moths. As hieroglyph carvers discovered, wasp wing number is sometimes difficult to appreciate – front and back wings are coupled together by a row of microscopic hooks, the hamulus, linking them into a unified aerofoil. The Hymenoptera is clearly a natural insect grouping; it includes the honeybees, bumblebees and ants, and a vast array of tiny or obscure creatures which never quite acquired helpful or usable common names. The problem is that, with the exception of a very small number of bees and ants, almost all of the insects in the Hymenoptera (something in the order of 250,000 species worldwide) are now also, quite legitimately, called 'wasps' by expert and non-expert alike.[3]

The smallest free-living insects (body lengths down to 0.139 mm), which parasitize insect eggs, are called fairy wasps for their pale flimsy appearance. The small ant-like insects that develop inside bizarre plant growths like oak apples and marble galls are called gall wasps. The slim, but often large, parasitoids that lay their eggs in caterpillars (the hatching maggots consume their victim, alive, from the inside) are routinely called ichneumon wasps – an ancient Greek coining, meaning 'tracker'. Elsewhere there are plenty of other wasps: potter wasps make small vase-shaped cells of mud in which they place paralysed insect prey for their grubs; mason wasps dig small burrows into lime mortar between old brickwork; fig wasps, tiny ant-like insects, specialize in fertilizing fig flowers; sabre wasps are large but slim insects with frighteningly long, sword-like tails; wood wasps are named for the giant intimidating adults and wood-boring grubs. Wasps, it seems, come in all shapes and sizes. No wonder people are baffled.

Despite this potential confusion, simplicity can still be brought to bear. The wasps buzzing around the remains of a cream tea are mostly easily identifiable to one particular insect group. In scientific terms they belong to the hymenopteran family *Vespidae*,[4] typically in the genera *Vespa*, *Vespula*, *Dolichovespula* or similar, and are described by entomologists as social wasps, or in North America in particular as yellow-jackets. Alongside these are the so-called paper wasps, *Polistes*, rather slimmer and longer-legged than yellow-jackets; they are named for their small papery nests, although as it turns out all vespids make nests from paper. In the British Isles there are currently ten species in this group, in Europe twenty species, twenty in North America and about 4,000 across the globe. These vespid hymenopterans now give us a focus, and the *Wasp* of this book's title.

Despite narrowing down the wasp concept to a manageable bookful, there is still every chance to stumble. Many a tabloid picture editor has fallen foul of expected taxonomic rigour by choosing an inappropriate image of a bee or fly, or one of those many non-vespine hymenopterans to match the carefully crafted nonsense about wasp plagues, foreign super-stinger invaders and bee-killers. So, for their benefit, at least, here are some further guidelines on what exactly a 'true' wasp looks like.

Within the insect order Hymenoptera, wasps (along with bees, ants and many of those parasitic ichneumons) are placed in the suborder Apocrita, from the Greek (*apokrisis*), meaning separated. Members of this large suborder have a narrow wasp-waist clearly separating thorax and abdomen (the petiole in entomological jargon), a structural feature that will later be personified in the extreme corsetry of Victorian women's fashion. This cutting-in of the narrow waist meant that wasps were sometimes referred to as 'cut-wasts' or, more tellingly, 'cut-wasted vermine as are winged'.[5] This narrow, sometimes stalk-like hinge allows the insect the most supreme flexibility in pointing its sting-tipped abdomen in almost any direction it likes – left, right, upwards or curled down underneath its body and pointing forward between its legs. This is especially helpful when the wasp is grappling with then paralysing its chosen caterpillar victim, or killing its insect prey. Picked up in animal paw, bird beak or between human finger and thumb it can use its manoeuvrability to manipulate its venomous tail and stab its attacker in the nearest available soft spot. Ouch.

The Apocrita is further subdivided, and within it the familiar assemblage of bees, wasps and ants are gathered into a natural evolutionary group – the Aculeata. This is an old and well-worn name deriving from the insect's obviously acutely pointed tail end, usually tipped with that familiar painful sting – the Aculeus of scientific textbooks.[6] Structural, behavioural and genetic similarities show these groups of insects to be intimately related, and clearly derived from a common ancestor dating to around 175–200 million years ago (MYA). To date, compression fossils, from Jurassic silt deposits in Central Asia, from perhaps some 150 MYA, contain what are thought to be the most ancient putative Aculeates.[7] These small insects from the extinct family Bethylonymidae have simple wing venation and slim ant-like bodies and seem closest to the modern family Bethylidae. There is no accepted common name for this obscure group of tiny insects, but they have short stings with which they subdue their prey. Fossils (in stone and in amber) recognizable as belonging to the modern lineages of bees, ants and wasps date from the early Cretaceous – about 135 MYA. The oldest known apparent true vespine wasp fossil appears to be *Palaeovespa baltica* from Baltic amber, calculated to be about 30 million years old.[8]

Ants seem relatively distinct from wasps. They are generally small and rather ant-like, with large triangular head, narrow thorax and bulbous abdomen. Worker ants' lack of wings makes their identification easy, but flying ants (winged males and queens) can sometimes be disconcertingly wasp-like. However, few ants are large or brightly coloured black and yellow. Confounding some wasps and bees, though, is a mistake still made even by expert naturalists.

The most straightforward distinction, but perhaps the one most difficult to discern from a photograph or a museum specimen, is that bees are wholly vegetarian – they and their larvae feed solely on carbohydrate sugary nectar and protein-rich pollen. This simple fact of ecology is partly at the root of the cult of honey, that magical sweet liquor that has fascinated and fixated humans for millennia and made bees the heroes that wasps are not. Bees are valued as pollinators and their earnest, businesslike diligence and industry further cements their good reputation. Wasps, on the other hand, are primarily predatory. Though they might

Selection of wasps, including the common wasp (*Vespa vulgaris*), hornet (*Vespa crabro*), red wasp (*Vespula rufa*) and one of the solitary mason wasps (*Ancistrocerus parietum*). From George Shaw and Frederick Nodder, *The Naturalist's Miscellany* (1810).

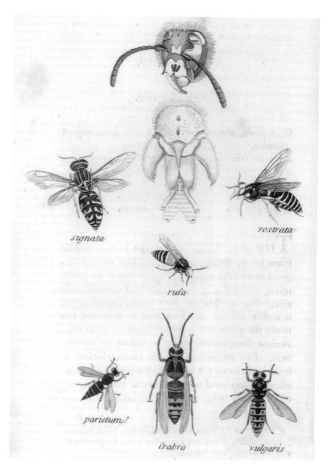

signata

rostrata

rufa

parietum?

Crabra

vulgaris

sometimes visit flowers for a bit of nectar and fallen fruit for juices, they must catch and kill insect prey to feed to their wholly carnivorous grubs back in the nest. They are not above ripping bits of decaying flesh from carrion, and will also scavenge gristly remnants from animal scats – all behaviours likely to alienate them further. There is a bizarre tale of wasps apparently chewing off small portions of live pigs' ears in the farmyard, and Canadian entomologist John Phipps claimed blood-stained Kleenex evidence when one chewed his ear ('fairly painful') before making off with a droplet of his blood.[9] Bees would never do anything as vulgar as this.

Structurally there are several very subtle differences between bees and wasps, but caution and a microscope are usually required to discern them. Colours and patterns are useless, with both groups varying through entire spectrums from striped to monochrome black, through various white-, yellow-, red- and orange-marked designs. Likewise, size ranges overlap completely, as do short- or long-leggedness, body proportions and wing shape. Although microscopic examination of wing venation patterns often shows unique layouts for some species there is no easy differentiation between wasps and bees.

The supposed hairiness of bees, often portrayed incorrectly on honey jars, really holds firm only for the cuddly bumbles; there are plenty of sleek, shining, almost bald bees, and under a microscope most wasps show off plenty of sensory hairs on their bodies. However, the structure of the hairs *is* a useful characteristic. Bees, even the shiniest and smoothest, will have a few hairs around the wing bases, and crucially these hairs are feathery up the stalk. Wasp bristles are never plumose, they are always plain and simple cylindrical shafts. The significance is that the branched bee hairs are good at accumulating pollen, the microscopic spheres of which become lodged in the fleecy strands. It is this adaptation

The hamulus, the series of hooks by which front (B) and hind (A) wings are attached together to form a single aerodynamic blade, ably decorated down the eye-piece by the Hon. Mrs Ward in *The Microscope* (1880).

that made bees the pollinating herbivores we know and love today. Even this character is variable, and some of the earliest bee fossils, beautifully preserved in amber, show a mixture of straight wasp hairs and plumed bee hairs. There is, in fact, still a very good scientific argument for claiming that bees are, after all, just a group of specialized pollen-feeding wasps.

But this is going backwards a little bit. On the whole the social wasps are distinct enough, and although it is sometimes difficult to describe that distinction simply, in concise terms and easy words, they have a 'look' to them – otherwise how could that black-and-yellow warning become so well known and so pervasive? The caveat must always be, though, that just because an insect is black-and-yellow patterned this does not automatically make it a wasp.

WHY DOES IT HURT SO?

The wasp sting is no casual dagger, it is a complicated piece of biological machinery. The main parts of its construction are paired penetrating stylets, an inner cylindrical venom tube and associated outer protective sheaths. The two minutely barbed lancets rapidly vibrate, sawing back and forth much in the manner of electric carving knife blades, puncturing and penetrating the flesh, whilst a muscular venom sac squeezes the poison from the glandular reservoir down the hollow hypodermic core.

Wasp venom is a highly complex cocktail of many different chemicals, including: protein-destroying enzymes to rupture flesh and blood cells; histamines to increase blood flow and spread pain; and neurotransmitters to confuse and over-stimulate nerves to the point of numbing pins and needles. Although it almost certainly first evolved to kill invertebrate prey, wasp toxin is also very toxic to higher organisms like birds and mammals (including us). The chemistry of wasp stings is remarkably uniform across various wasp groups, and similarities with bee venom again show a common ancestor not too far off. It's a nice story, but Aristotle was seriously misled by the alchemical beliefs of his age when he thought the wasps of Naxos had even more deadly stings since they were reputed to feed on the flesh of adders.

The agonizing pain from a single wasp sting, say 15 µg of venom (that's about $1/65,000$g), is testament to its chemical potency. Multiple stings produce severe local swelling, redness, generalized nausea, vomiting, wheezing, confusion and dizziness, and can cause kidney and liver damage. Half a dozen stings and the victim will almost certainly need a sit down with a cup of tea. With fifty to a hundred stings the casualty should seek immediate medical attention. There is no antivenom, such as is used against snakebites, but dialysis can remove toxins from the blood to prevent any long-term organ damage. An average person weighing

The weapon in question, an extruded wasp sting – the Aculeus. Smooth and shining to penetrate its victim easily, the tip is also minutely barbed, though not as strongly as in the famously hooked honeybee sting.

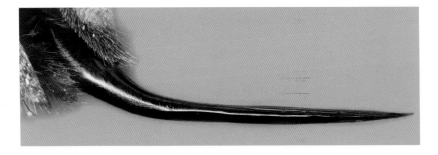

Away from the danger end of the wasp, the tongue is another miracle of engineering, complete with several sets of articulated palps to help manipulate food and paper pulp. As revealed to an eager populace by Jabez Hogg in *The Microscope* (1886).

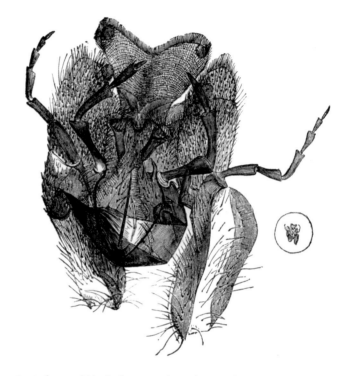

60–85 kg would be lucky to survive a thousand stings. There are regular reports of deaths after 1,200 stings, but one victim survived 2,243.[10] Pliny the Elder claimed that 27 hornet stings were enough to kill a human. Such exactitude is mere dogma, and other claims were made that 'nine of their stings will kill a man, and three times nine will be able to kill a strong horse'. Seventeenth-century Dutch scientist Jan Swammerdam sceptically reported that 'it is a common observation among the vulgar that six hornets are sufficient to kill a horse'.[11] With the hindsight of modern medicine we can now dismiss all this as superstitious nonsense, particularly as things became supposedly worse 'at the rising of the dog-star [in summer], and after, at which time they have a more fiery, hasty, and inflaming nature, and men at that season, by reason of their large exaltation and sending forth of spirits, grow more weak and faint'.[12] Envenomation from wasp stings is still not an exact science, and much depends on the precise doses injected by one or more wasps, and the varied responses from different sizes, ages and vigour of the victims – dog-star season notwithstanding. Multiple stings can be very dangerous and most reports are from agricultural workers caught out in the open. There is a report, from the mid-twentieth century, that a farmer ploughing a field in Israel hit a large subterranean wasps' nest; he understandably fled, but his mule, trapped in the harness, died from the stings it sustained from the wasps, angry at having their home destroyed.[13]

Seventeenth-century naturalist and philosopher Edward Topsell wrote about wasps, and although most of it is decanted directly from classical Greco-Roman, medieval and early Renaissance sources, he introduced a few personal observations, including a vicious attack on a defenceless sparrow:

> I my self being at Duckworth in Huntingdonshire, my native soyle, I saw on a time a great wasp or hornet making after, and fiercely pursuing a sparrow in the open street of the town, who at length was wounded with her sting, was presently cast to the ground, the hornet satisfying her self with the sucked blood of her quelled prey, to the exceeding admiration of all the beholders and considerers of this seldom seen combate.[14]

We need to be careful believing what is written though. In the 1658 reprint of Topsell's great book *The History of Four-footed Beasts and Serpents*, the first English translation of Thomas Muffet's *Theatre of*

Insects is also included as an appendix. In it, Muffet (1553–1604) gives almost exactly the same anecdote, virtually word for word, but this time it is purported to be Pennius (co-author Thomas Penny) who observed the sparrow attack in the wide and open street in Peterborough. At least Peterborough is still identifiable in a modern gazetteer, whereas no Duckworth is currently known within Huntingdonshire or without, and it is likely that Topsell was writing about Buckworth, about 15 km south of Peterborough, which surely he would have spelled correctly if it had been his native soil. Sparrows are small birds and hornets are large wasps, but this sensational tale now rings hollow.

According to Plutarch, Cleopatra was fascinated by poisons, and tested various venoms, including (supposedly) that from wasps, to kill condemned prisoners. This topic was the inspiration for French artist Alexandre Cabanel's 1887 oil painting showing a languid Cleopatra luxuriating on a bed of tiger skins

Rousing from hibernation, a queen wasp takes a moment to groom herself in the warm sun; though not as fluffy as a bumble she is still relatively hirsute.

while a priest-like official has just administered something from a glass phial to a figure writhing on the ground clutching his belly in agony; a discarded metal chalice lies on the floor nearby. Of course wasp venom given orally would have little effect on the human body; the complex sting proteins would simply be digested and neutralized by the stomach enzymes. The haemolytic, inflammatory and neurotoxic chemicals need to be given as direct injection into the flesh or bloodstream to have their effect. It seems unlikely that either ancient Greeks or Egyptians could have achieved this with wasps – true hypodermics did not appear until the seventeenth century. An unfortunate cross-phylum taxonomic mix-up between wasps and asps also seems to have been garbled into various English translations and commentaries on Plutarch over the last 150 years, not helped by enthusiastic but ill-informed Internet search engines. Cleopatra famously (or at least apocryphally) died from an asp bite, but this is unlikely to have been the asp we know today (*Vipera aspis*, a relative of the venomous but hardly deadly European adder), nor a wasp, but rather the Egyptian cobra sometimes given as 'aspis' in old texts. Wasp, asp or aspis venom, Cabanel's depiction of oral administration does not stand up to scrutiny, nor does Plutarch's narrative. And the tale of Cleopatra's macabre fascination with death by wasp must remain tantalizingly speculative still.

Having said this, even without direct injection, it is still just about possible that wasp sting deaths could have been deliberately orchestrated. In the fourth century AD Marcus, Bishop of Arethusa (in modern-day Syria) destroyed a heathen temple, and was martyred by a pagan mob who smeared his body with honey and strung him up in a basket to be stung to death by wasps. Shakespeare may have been recalling this anecdote (*The Winter's Tale*, IV.4) when he has Autolycus suggest: 'He has a son, who shall be flayed alive; then 'nointed over with honey, set on the head of a wasp's nest; then stand till he be three quarters and a dram dead.' Autolycus is variously described as a vagabond, a roguish peddler and a pickpocket, and his character delights in bawdy songs and bloodthirsty threats. Threat is about as near to danger as this particular scenario gets. Being smeared with honey and tied down to stakes in the ground is a well-rehearsed Hollywood tableau, usually in association with ants' nests. Yet it is more fictional literary trope than factual reality.

Back in the real world, Swiss physician and naturalist Conrad Gessner (1516–1565) reported a woman dying from a single sting in the throat; swelling of the soft tissues at the back of the mouth probably blocked her windpipe causing her to asphyxiate. This was exactly what Topsell described nearly a century later:

> a poor woman . . . being extremely thirsty . . . finding by chance a black jack or tankard on the table in the hall, she very inconsiderately and rashly set it to her mouth, never suspecting or looking what might be in it, and suddenly a wasp in her greediness passed down with the drink and stinging her, there immediately came a great tumour in her throat . . . so that her breath being interceded, the miserable wretch . . . fell down and dyed.[15]

Anyone who has ever been stung on the lips or tongue will testify to the alarming amount of swelling that occurs, and the serious consequences of being stung in the mouth are emphasized in all modern medical information about wasps. Unfortunately it is these rare and unusual events that flavour the human understanding of wasps and fuel the myth factory that gives them their bad reputation.

The pain from a wasp sting is usually described as sudden, stabbing, sharp, often hot or burning, and likened to lemon

A rather fanciful illustration from Henry Southwell's *New Book of Martyrs* (1765). Despite the look of a gentle garden swing, Bishop Marcus's torture device came complete with wasps.

juice or vinegar spilled onto an open cut, leaving the wound smarting and sore. Shakespeare, in *The Winter's Tale*, likens 'wasp tails' to goads, thorns and nettles, all equally familiar sources of stinging pain, as relevant now as it was to a then still very rural Elizabethan society.

Strangely, literature is short on precise descriptive evocations of wasp-sting pain, and more often it is other types of hurt or tissue damage that are likened to stings. This is presumably because most people have not been stabbed with acid-dipped daggers or branded with red-hot pokers, but almost all will have been stung by a wasp at some point.

Perhaps a warning not to use sweet-smelling sunscreen. The flying insects look rather bumble-like, but the joke, in well-worn silly postcard style, works nevertheless.

This lack of precise descriptive prose has opened the way to more imaginative fantasies, like the portrayal of hallucinogenic venom from the genetically engineered wasps, 'tracker jackers' (a play on yellow-jacket) in the dystopian *Hunger Games* series. Pus-oozing welts the size of oranges and wild delirium are described, along with psychotropic and memory-altering side effects, paralysis, convulsions and death.

ACID OR ALKALI?

Ever since the first wasp stung the first Australopithecus, humans have been looking for an easy and immediate remedy to the sudden stabbing pain. Nicander, Pliny and Aristotle proposed a whole range from the soothing balm of crushed herbs, salt and vinegar, to the bizarre practice of wearing the bill of a woodpecker around the neck, or part of an owl. Verbal spells and chants are widely mentioned – the modern equivalent might be swearing loudly to feel a bit better.

Ibn al-Jazzar, writing in the ninth century, suggested a poultice of henna and barley meal, or milk of figs, pounded walnuts, seaweeds and vinegar, and various other herbal concoctions. In the late fifteenth century, the *Hortus Sanitatis* (Garden of Health) suggested a 'plaster made of wilde malowe leaves is good to draw out the stinge. The donge of a goose draweth out the venyme of any wasps. And salt and vinegar tempered with hony is very good. Oyle of bay is good also for the stynge.'[16] Folk preparations still claimed to be efficacious today include dripping vinegar on the wound or dousing it with bicarbonate of soda, to counteract the sting's supposed alkali or acid base. The venom is neither (its pH of 6.8 is so close to the neutral 7 of pure water that it makes no odds), but the astringent smart of vinegar or soda lime on an open cut is a sting so familiar that many imagine a pseudo-scientific association. It did not help that early dissections of wasp stings often – wrongly – labelled the venom sac as an 'acid gland'. Some ants, however, produce formic acid (chemically very similar to acetic acid vinegar), but they tend to spray it as an aerosol defence, rather than inject it through a stinger hypodermic tube.

From the Middle Ages onwards, the numerous ingredients for ointments suggested included marsh-mallow (the plant not the confectionery), willow leaves, rue, marjoram, grape juice, lemon juice, wild cucumber seeds, honey, wine, mud, cow's blood and cow dung. Like dock leaves smeared as a remedy against nettle stings, these all probably worked by cooling and calming the skin. Sometimes the nest combs or the wasps themselves were an ingredient in the potion – a sort of bastardized homoeopathic retribution extracted from the perpetrators of the pain.

When William Hutton wrote *To Miss P – Whose Lip was Stung by a Wasp* (1793), he suggested a kiss on the lips might help:

A remedy you want that cures
Then let my lips be joined to yours.
Balsamic virtues may be found,
Sufficient for the deeper wound.[17]

The idea of vinegar, balsamic or otherwise, sweeping away the
pain may be connected with its likely antiseptic qualities; it was
a fermented post-alcoholic brew in an age when most drinking
water was of doubtful purity.

Widely promoted 'natural remedies' still used by some include
rubbing the sting site with garlic, pasting on honey or holding a
slice of lemon, cucumber or onion against the pain. None of these
seem to have any scientific basis other than a general cooling
sensation against the hotness of the wound. Over-the-counter
pharmaceutical preparations containing antihistamines may
help in the long term to reduce swelling, but any pain relief is
probably just from the cool unguent ointment and a gentle mas-
saging. For simple wasp stings current medical advice is to remove
any part of the sting mechanism still attached to the skin, wash
the wound with soap and water, apply a cold compress (cold
water on a flannel, or an ice pack), avoid scratching and put away
that balsamic vinegar and baking soda.

Ironically, some stings actually seem to counter other types of
pain. Since Hippocrates and Pliny, there have been anecdotal
reports of bee-keepers finding release from arthritis aches after
regular stings on their hands. Results of scientific studies on deliberate sting infliction to treat the disease have been equivocal, but
sporadic self-medication continues to be reported.[18] Similar anecdotes about accidental wasp stings alleviating rheumatoid or
osteoarthritis, carpel tunnel syndrome and swollen hands
abound, but medical opinion seems to take a harsher view when
bees are not involved. There have been reports that wasp (and

honeybee) stings lead directly to osteoarthritis, and there is always the background fear that repeated stings can cause sensitization, leading to greater than normal bodily responses, culminating in the potential for anaphylactic shock. The general consensus is that nobody would deliberately allow themselves to be stung by wasps.

This has not deterred u.s. entomologist Justin Schmidt, who has developed a carefully scaled pain index to cover all insect stings.[19] He didn't set out to get himself deliberately stung, but his studies across the Hymenoptera have often brought him closer to his subjects then comfort might ordinarily allow, and he has taken to the task of documenting the various toxins' effects with gusto. At its gentlest, pain level 1 covers the stings of most ants and small bees; the sting of the sweat bee is 'light, ephemeral,

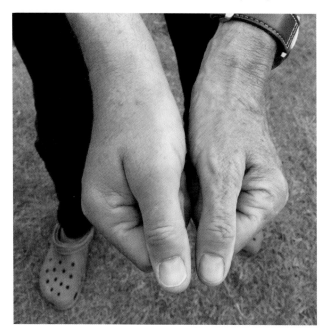

The trials and tribulations of gardening without gloves near a wasp nest. One hand wrinkled and drawn, the other plump and smooth.

almost fruity; a tiny spark has just singed a single hair on your arm'. Our *Vespula* social wasps come it at pain level 2: 'hot and smoky, almost irreverent; imagine W. C. Fields extinguishing a cigar on your tongue'. Hornets, most other social wasps, bumble-bees, fire ants and honeybees also come into this broad bracket, suggesting that this is perhaps the baseline venom strength from which others have evolved. Incidentally, Aristotle claimed that wasp stings were more painful than those of honeybees, although he does not elucidate much in the way of a numerical comparison. Schmidt's pain level 3 includes some paper wasps, *Polistes* species and velvet ants (family Mutillidae), which are actually a type of wasp in the narrow sense even though they are furry and wing-less: 'after eight hours of unrelenting drilling into that ingrown toenail, you find the drill wedged into the toe'. His highest distress is reserved for the few species according pain level 4, including the bullet ant (a real ant this time), tarantula hawk (a type of spider-hunting wasp) and the vespine warrior wasp, *Synoeca sep-tentrionalis*, about which he writes: 'Torture. You are chained in the flow of an active volcano. Why did I start this list?'

DO ALL WASPS STING?

So, to recapitulate. Wasps sting. Except, of course, not all of them do. Many of the smaller wasps in the broadest sense (those gall wasps, fig wasps and many diminutive solitary species) are just too slight, and their sting mechanisms too feeble to penetrate human skin to get any venom through. These can be picked up with impunity by the hymenopterist. But even large yellow-jackets and hornets have their stingless forms. It is a biological fact beyond dispute that the stinging mechanism is part of the egg-laying apparatus, hence only females can sting. There is only small comfort to take from this biological certainty, however, for the vast majority of the nest occupants are female. The many thousands of foraging workers are females, and even though they do not have properly developed ovaries and do not lay eggs, they all have the accompanying egg-associated equipment in their abdomens, and the sting is a well-developed part of this.

Ironically, the idea of masculine aggression, strength and power in all creatures is so deeply ingrained in our society that the harmlessness of male wasps is a fact often lost. Even *Far Side* cartoonist Gary Larson, who specializes in entomological humour, gets it wrong when he shows a white-coat-clad medical doctor pressing his ear up against the breast-plate of a worried-looking medieval knight in armour: 'Ooo! You're right, Sir Dwayne! If I knock right here, I can make him start buzzing . . . Ooo, and he's angry!' In fact Gary, he's harmless. Sometimes called drones (but that name's really for male honeybees), male wasps have no weapon. Given reasonable certainly that you have sexed the animal correctly (slightly longer antennae with thirteen rather than twelve segments, and seven rather than six abdominal segments, but be careful), they can be gently held between forefinger and

Head of a North American paper wasp, *Polistes metricus*, clearly showing the 12 antennal segments of a female, large eyes and toothed chewing jaws.

thumb, to the wonder and awe of the uninitiated. Lack of a weapon doesn't stop him wriggling, and in a superb example of desperate bluff, the male wasp actively tries to startle its would-be assailant by jabbing and stabbing the offending fingers with its blunt tail-tip, as if it had a sting inside. But to no avail.

> A wasp with no sting in his tail,
> Was considered by all a bit frail.
> Unlike a sister,
> Innocuous mister –
> The fate of a *Vespula* male.[20]

2 Warning Colours

Typically, strongly contrasting flashes of black and yellow are a stark warning; the message 'do not touch' is loud and clear. A walk down any busy shopping street will soon show scaffolding poles spiralled with black-and-yellow tape indicating an obvious bump hazard. The entrance to a low bridge is emphasized by alternating black and yellow blockwork. This colour scheme is especially designed to catch our attention. The international standard for warning and danger signs, whether from electric shock, slippery floors or explosive materials, is crisp black against a sulphurous yellow. That our eyes are programmed to respond to this colour scheme is entirely natural, even though black-and-yellow flashes, dashes or stripes are not common in nature, which is mostly dominated by brown earth, green leaves and blue sky. Black-and-yellow warning signs are a direct result of our fear of stinging insects – wasps in particular.

The evolutionary significance of black-and-yellow warning colours started long before humans and their potential pedestrian bumps or vehicle crashes. Although unclear from the now earthen-coloured fossil record, these contrasting patterns probably began as mammal, bird and small dinosaur avoidance tactics perhaps 125–150 million years ago. Assuming a visual acuity at least broadly similar to modern animals, these primordial predators would have paid special heed to any strikingly marked insects

that stung if they attempted to eat them or raid their nests, and they would have avoided them next time round. So why black and yellow and not, say, black and white?

COLOUR BARS

Black and yellow are, at least, naturally occurring colours in insects – respectively produced by melanin and carotenoids. These are pretty ubiquitous chemical pigments across almost all living organisms, an indication that they evolved long before the need for sting warnings. White, on the other hand is an uncommon feature in animals, usually not produced by albino lack of pigment, but by complex microscopic light-scattering substructures in the integument. White appears to have evolved separately in mammals, birds and various insect groups on separate rare occasions back in deep prehistory. Black and yellow, on the other hand, had a head start, a common ancestry, by many hundreds of millions of years.

Once a vague propensity to develop blotches, streaks, bars or stripes had appeared, the enhancement of larger neighbouring solid blocks of increasingly dense bright colour is, intuitively, a simple process of emphasis through genetic variation and evolutionary selection. Once this got started, there was a reinforcing of the colour scheme as potential predators began to understand the association of sudden intense pain with the black-and-yellow pattern schemes of the pain-givers. Today many different wasp groups are black and yellow, but this is not just a casual continuation of some ancient trait: there is a constraining selective pressure to keep to more or less the same colours and patterns, rather than each group diverging off to evolve new designs. This reinforcement occurs across very broad taxonomic boundaries, which is why many bumblebees, solitary bees, spider-hunting

German-born naturalist Maria Sibylla Merian (1647–1717) is renowned for the painstaking colour plates with which she illustrated her life-cycle studies of South American butterflies and moths. The wasp is a possible predator she observed, but is rather stylized.

Nam gentem' super gentem Exurgere, eal umq Spe'
ſuram telluris infiſte Re-plos iam in noſtris tribulanonibus Ver,
uimbs, Quam in Co Dicibus legimus Quam te Kremotus
erbes inumeras ſubruat ex Alijs mun ti partibus,
icitis Quia frequenter AuDimus peſtilenti am Et

wasps and ichneumons are also bright black and yellow. They all gain protection by combining their individual warning/pain associations to predators, and gaining security and safety in numbers. Called Müllerian mimicry, after the German naturalist Fritz Müller (1821–1897), who first postulated the idea in 1878,[1] it explains why even very rare black-and-yellow hymenopterans gain protection, even though there may not be enough of them to teach the important stinging lessons to predators in the first place. They just tailgate on the painfully learned lessons given earlier by the common black-and-yellow species in the area. Just as humans only need to learn the black-and-yellow warning sign code once, predators have no need to learn to identify every different creature that might have a sting.

Wariness of buzzing insects is an adjunct to the human avoidance of wasps. In truth, the vibration of wasp wings is at the low and soft end of the decibel scale, but this has not stopped wild over-exaggeration through history. Both Edward Topsell and Thomas Muffet summarize wasp buzzing – Topsell first: 'as bees do, but more fearful, hideous, terrible, and whistling, especially when they are provoked to wrath'.[2] Muffet continues by quoting Theocritus: 'in comparison of a bawling idiot, to a man of learning ... The buzzing of a wasp against the grasshopper.'[3]

DANGER BY DEFAULT

This emphasis of black and yellow by association continues today, in the human mind, which is why every depiction of wasps in art, literature, song and commerce is a default black and yellow. In fact it seems obligatory to call any so-coloured man-made object 'wasp'. The Bachmann series of short wheelbase diesel railway locomotives were called wasps purely on the basis of the hi-vis black-and-yellow warning chevrons front and back.

A potter wasp is one of the delicate elements of illumination which Flemish painter Joris Hoefnagel (1542–1601) added to the exquisite calligraphy of Georg Bocskay (d. 1575) in *Mira Calligraphiae Monumenta* (Model Book of Calligraphy), though the wing number seems incorrect.

Likewise the Marmon Wasp acquired its appellation for its vespine colour scheme, although its victory in the first Indianapolis 500 automobile race in 1911 may also have reflected its aggressive tenacity and buzzing engine. Elsewhere the wasp synthesizer has a quirky 1970s keyboard with black and yellow keys, rather than the usual black and white; various wasp motorcycles are prominently black and yellow; and of course the Hyper Wasp yoyo was also appropriately coloured. It is probably contrived, but the A-WASP (Acoustic Warning Signal Projector) sonic repellent device for riot police, an oversized super-powerful directional megaphone siren, is threateningly black-and-yellow barred, to look suitably weapon-like in the face of a braying crowd. It is perhaps slightly disappointing that Wasp Barcode Technologies does not promote black-and-yellow product scan displays for groceries being tallied at the supermarket checkout.

Oddly, the vigilante-cum-superhero Green Hornet (launched originally on radio in 1938) was not at all wasp-coloured, but rather demure in a secretive disguise of long green overcoat, fedora and face mask. Perhaps a striking yellow-and-black outfit was deemed too brazen for a crime fighter mostly lurking in the shadows. At least Captain Hornet (appeared in 35 issues of British boys' magazine *The Hornet* during the 1960s) had a bright red uniform and flew a black-and-yellow spaceship-type vehicle.

MISTAKEN IDENTITY

A wasp logo is now an amorphous and nebulous design, with varying numbers of wings and an uncertain number of legs, perfectly exemplified in those first ancient Egyptian hieroglyphs. All it needs to get the message across is a vaguely flexible pointed tail and some black-and-yellow styling. It's easy for the pedant entomologist to get frustrated at this seeming anatomical ignorance, but humans are not the only ones to get confused, and having your identity mistaken for a wasp is an important survival tactic across many insect orders.

What better way to avoid being attacked than to convince any would-be attacker that you are actually armed and dangerous? So it is with so many harmless yet menacingly coloured wasp-mimicking insects. Wasp longhorn beetles (family Cerambycidae) emphasize their disguise by flying readily from flower to flower. Clear-wing moths (family Sesiidae) have narrow clear membranous, almost scale-free wings and slim black and yellow barred bodies, often with a dark saddle patch on each side at the base of the abdomen to give the impression of that flexible wasp waist. Supreme, though, among wasp lookalikes are the true flies (Diptera), with bold yellow-barred patterns regularly appearing among a multitude of soldier flies (aquatic larvae, family Stratiomyidae), robber flies (insect predators, family Asilidae), and hoverflies (predatory, scavenging or plant-feeding larvae, family Syrphidae).

This last group, the hoverflies, are so numerous, so diverse and so obvious in their brazen flower-visiting habits that they are endlessly mistaken for wasps (a few are also superb bumblebee or honeybee mimics). The variety of their colour patterns is astonishing – usually black with endless variations on yellow, cream or pale orange bars, dots, dashes, flecks, broad and narrow bands shaped like paired golf clubs, moustaches, commas and chevrons. The success of their wide-ranging but obviously wasp-like colour schemes is directly ascribed to their close resemblance to wasps. Batesian mimcry is named after the Victorian naturalist Henry Walter Bates (1825–1892), who first proposed that harmless insects gained protection from attack by their close resemblance to dangerous stinging or poisonous models.[4] So good is this mimicry that it is often possible to align individual hoverfly species with particular wasp species occurring in the same area.[5]

Hoverflies are also very easy to photograph because they suck up pollen or drink down nectar in a much more leisurely way than either bees or wasps. Consequently, it is their mistaken images that frequently adorn newspaper or web reports on wasps. The confusion between wasps, bees and flies has a convoluted and chequered history, and just as early writers did not necessarily know the precise scientific distinction between these different groups of insects, so too have illustrators and commentators down the centuries been muddled and confused.

Not wasps, but startling mimics. Left: *Volucella zonaria*, a striking hornet-like hoverfly. Right: *Rutpela maculata*, the wasp longhorn.

WASPS IN ART – FINE, AND LESS THAN FINE

In early paintings especially, some care has to be taken when trying to interpret 'wasps', because the default buzzing stinging insect is most likely to be a bee. The exuberant, bizarre, amusing, sometimes vulgar but always fascinating medieval manuscript marginalia mostly show honeybees since these were important semi-domesticated animals at the time, honey providing just about the only sweetness for foods. Though it is difficult to guess

One of a series of trading cards issued by German shoe-polish and footwear company Erdal, *c.* 1928, demonstrating mimicry, in this case *Polistes* paper wasps (1) and a *Chrysotoxum* hoverfly (2).

A sublimely subtle and beautiful glass pendent by René Lalique, *c.* 1920. Before his fame with moulded glass, Lalique was a jewellery designer and often used black-and-yellow wasps in gaudy pieces.

from the highly stylized image, there are reckoned to be several wasps on the finely illuminated capital letter C of a famous collection of late thirteenth-century French poems *Fables of the Court*.[6] It illustrates the fable of the wolf, and of the beetle which climbs up its backside; a battle between various forest animals and insects rallying to the insulted beetle's cause results in a deer being stung by a wasp. Though delightfully painted, the wasps are little more than winged blobs that could equally be bees, birds or bats, were it not for the text naming them as the vespine warriors that eventually win the day.

The extended fifteenth-century herbal, bestiary and life manual *Hortus Sanitatis* crudely figures wasps (probably more tree-familiar hornets rather than yellow-jackets) flying around a decrepit bole, but a few pages earlier an almost identical woodcut shows honeybees flying round a hole in a large tree where a feral colony has been established.[7] During the medieval period, these illustrations were meant more for decoration rather than as an identification guide, and their execution is stylized by tradition as well as lack of close observation on the part of the artists.

Not all wasp depictions are so bluntly careless. Even to the untrained eye wasps are beautifully coloured and delicately patterned, and as artistic techniques became more sophisticated, better and clearer representations of wasps become more obvious. There is a fine, if not necessarily regular, tradition of illustrating wasps in Western art after the Renaissance, particularly during the height of the still-life genre in Holland and the Low Countries in the seventeenth to nineteenth centuries. Good examples appear in works by Balthasar van der Ast

Almost identical and highly stylized illustrations from the *Hortus sanitatis* (1491), purportedly showing bees (left) and wasps (right) nesting in hollow trees. The unusual and startling colouring was probably added at a later date by the book's owner.

One of very many tulip compositions by Jacob Marrel, showing a wasp (centre right), along with other decorative flourishes; 1636. These were almost certainly painted from dead specimens – clues are in the curl of the dragonfly tail and overdramatic lizard pose.

(1593/4–1657); in particular his *Variegated Tulips in a Ceramic Vase (with a Wasp, a Dragonfly, a Butterfly and a Lizard)* (1625) shows a fine *Vespula* sitting on the table, though the antennae look rather short and stout, possibly a result of his model being dead. His later *Still-life of Flowers, Shells and Insects* (1635) shows a clearly dead and curled *Vespula* wasp lying on its side at bottom right. There is a certain irony that Rachel Ruysch's *Rosenzweig mit Käfer und Biene* (Rose Branch with Beetle and Bee, 1741) appears to show a wasp rather than a bee. Other skilful depictions appear in works by Georg Flegel (1566–1638) whose *Still-life with Bread and Confectionary* (early seventeenth century) shows a huge hornet, and Jan van Huysum (1682–1749), although his *Vase of Flowers* (1722) shows a hoverfly, *Helophilus pendulus*.

According to art historians, these tiny details were allegorical motifs.[8] Fruits perhaps represent truth, salvation, wholesomeness and love. Flowers are claimed to represent different things with, for example, a rose signifying love, a lily purity and a sunflower devotion. Butterflies and bees perhaps represented hope, or brevity (of existence), but quite what other obscure creatures might stand for, including wasps, is uncertain beyond the usual nuisance notions of danger, pain, annoyance, theft or destruction. At the very least they showed the skill of the painters in combining

Study from the notebook of Jacob Marrel. The tulips are shown with delicate clarity, but the bumblebee and wasp, both with an uncertain number of legs. appear to be mating.

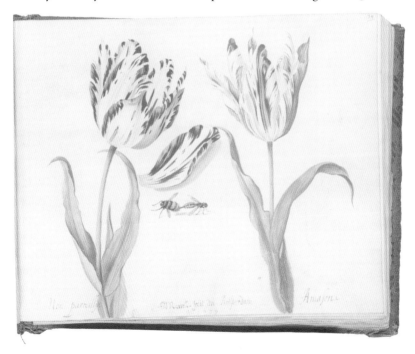

lifelike animals against the backdrops of colourful flowers and foliage, adding depth and layers of interest. Perhaps there was an I-spy aspect of hunt-the-tiny-insect in the complex forms and kaleidoscope colours – a kind of grand Dutch masters' entomological version of *Where's Wally?*

Jan van Kessel the Elder (1626–1679) painted endless depictions of insects in a huge series of famous nature-study tableaux, usually oil on copper panels used to decorate drawer sets and collectors' cabinets. These often featured a bizarre selection of obscure and seemingly unappealing creepy-crawlies including beetles, caterpillars, flies, leaf bugs, crickets and water insects, as

Not a wasp this time, but a wasp-mimic hoverfly (*Helophilus pendulus*) in a painting by Jan van Huysum, 1722.

Giovanna Garzoni, *Still-life with a Bowl of Citrons*, late 1640s. Though anatomically well depicted, a wasp would realistically only settle on an old, rotten or damaged lemon – not bright, fresh fruit in a bowl.

well as more usual subjects such as butterflies, moths and attractively patterned seashells. They were probably deliberately chosen for their off-beat curiosity value, since the point of cabinets of curiosity (sometimes 'cabinets of wonder') was to house wondrous and unusual objects from natural history. There are plenty of Van Kessel wasps, including several that are quite obviously *Vespula* yellow-jackets and also the common European hornet *Vespa crabro*. Alongside these are several nearly identifiable species of solitary wasps, ichneumons, bumblebees and mimics like wasp longhorns, bee chafer and hoverflies. There is often a somewhat stiff wings-splayed, legs-sprawled dead look about his insects, and it is quite likely that they were painted from specimens he himself had collected and which he brought out from his own cabinet of curiosities as needed for his various commissions. Occasionally some of his more flimsy-looking, delicate insects seem to lack definition, as if copied from copies of copies, but his wasps are crisp and clear; he must have had a good stash of them.

Illustration by Jan van Kessel showing a black-veined white butterfly, a garden tiger moth, earwigs, plant bugs and several other anatomically dubious insects, 17th century. The hornet, *Vespa crabro* (top left), is superbly depicted.

There is still every opportunity to fall into imprecision. The Goodhart collection of seventeenth-century English embroidered samplers, now housed at the National Trust's Montacute House in Somerset, has a selection of stylized and sometimes quite frankly imaginary creatures among more familiar decorations, but it includes at least one insect that appears more wasp than bee.

There is also a long tradition of fine naturalistic art in Japan and China, with many depictions of wasps alongside flowers and other animals. The famed printmaker Kitagawa Utamaro (*c.* 1754 –1806) produced a series of delightful woodblock prints of insects and other garden creatures (1788); the paper wasp (*hachi*) and hairy caterpillar (*kemushi*) are delicately and accurately portrayed against a backdrop of flowing leaves and tendrils with a large open area of white space in typical Japanese aesthetic. There is sometimes a playful juxtaposition. Ohara Kosun's 1935 *Monkey, Wasp and Persimmons* shows a small fluffy monkey reaching out

Border decoration from a 16th- or 17th-century embroidery sampler showing a wasp-type creature. The wings look un-anatomical, but the body shape, colours, leg and antennal details are all reminiscent of *Vespula*.

Study by Otto van Veen (*c.* 1556–1629) with a small tortoiseshell butterfly, its caterpillar, a rove beetle, a sawfly and, based on its relative size, the European hornet.

to pull down a branch to better get at the ripe fruit, but just in frame at the top of the picture the distinctive umbrella shape of a paper wasp nest and a resident wasp suggests a tantalizing danger should the animal disturb these notoriously defensive insects. His earlier *Wasps and Flowering Hortensia* (or hydrangeas, 1928) sets the beautifully delineated, but perhaps slightly menacing wasps against the soft familiarity of this garden plant. Nagamachi Chikuseki puts a wasp centrally in his early twentieth-century *Wasp and Grapes*. Here the contrast is between exact preciseness in the execution of the single brightly coloured wasp compared with the more free-flowing lines and the muted colours of the vine.

Polistes nest in a woodcut by Kubo Shunman (1757–1820). The title as suggested by the New York Metropolitan Museum of Art, 'Hives, with wasps, and a box with spoon for honey', is improbable given that hives and honey are associated only with honeybees; more likely the small nest was harvested for medicinal purposes, using the narrow-bladed knife.

A *Polistes* umbrella wasp nest among persimmon branches by Shibata Zeshin (1807–1891), skilfully painted in lacquer.

Scroll painting by unidentified Qing dynasty artist, possibly 17th or 18th century. Although most of the insects flying around the rose flowers are probably meant to be bees, a lone wasp waits in rather sinister fashion at the end of the flowing tendril . . . waiting to pounce?

Wasps and a hairy caterpillar on arrowroot by Kitagawa Utamaro (1753–1806). Despite its relatively large size, the caterpillar is in grave peril from the ferocious wasps.

Wasps – small, delicate, precisely shaped and coloured – also lent themselves to incorporation into the fine manufacturing arts that blossomed in the seventeenth- to nineteenth-century Japanese culture of the Edo period. They, and their nests, are regularly the subjects of exquisitely carved netsuke, lacquered inro, ceramics and cloisonné ware. Even sword-smiths worked them into the gold- and metalwork tsuba hand guards of the famous ceremonial and high-status weapon pieces of the samurai katana swords.

Arguably postage stamps are the modern equivalent of these small decorative pieces, and well-executed paintings of social wasps feature on the offerings from many parts of the world including Ascension Island, Australia, Bangladesh, Belarus, Canada, Ivory Coast, Nigeria, Pitcairn Islands, Rwanda and

Senegal. The only wasp to appear on a Royal Mail stamp in Britain is a rare, solitary mason wasp, *Pseudopipona herrichii*. It is rather pretty, but not one of the familiar yellow-jackets you'd be shooing off of your jam sandwiches.

The inclusion of wasps as decorative motifs blends with their symbolic significance in ancient and modern art. Hua Yan's *Album of Sketches from Life* (*c.* 1740), regarded as a masterpiece of Qing dynasty painting, contains a superbly executed paper wasp nest on a cassia branch, with the insects huddled around the comb exactly as they do in real life. Also in the series is the slightly comical *Wasp and Tiger*, where a skinny (old?) tiger raises its paw

Tsuba, a sword hand-guard, by Kano Natsuo (1828–1898), showing a carp leaping from the water to snatch at a passing wasp; or it could be a bee.

A cloissoné enamel vase, c. 1912–26, from the famous Japanese manufacturer Ando, decorated with a gold enamel wasp motif.

Polistes netsuke by Naitō Toyomasa (1773–1856). Although the hexagonal shape of the cells is lost, a realism is found in the depiction of the nearly full-grown grubs peeking out

to rub its nose; its sad expression and the wasp perched on a nearby stem clearly suggest that this mighty beast has been stung by the tiny insect. The traditional Chinese word for wasp is also applied to bees and hornets, and is a homophone for 'ennoblement'. Combined with a regal tiger the symbolism often means 'to advance in rank and position', perhaps a statement of power and aspiration. The comedy and sarcasm in Hua Yan's picture is quite different, and might reflect the artist's own thwarted ambitions. This theme, however, remains timeless, and is the topic of endless rather mawkish Western designs, postcards and pictures from the late nineteenth and early twentieth centuries showing overly cute kittens or puppies apparently fixated on a nearby wasp or bee. You just know what is going to happen, though you hope it won't.

3 It's in their Genes

At its height in mid-summer, a typical wasp nest as big as a beach ball may contain 3,000–6,000 individuals all engaged in frenetic activity – foraging for food, feeding the brood, collecting wood pulp, building combs, cleaning the nest, defending the colony. Over the short (usually about five to six months) span of the colony, upwards of 10,000–15,000 adult wasps will be produced from the brood combs.[1] Almost all of these wasps will be females. Only towards early autumn will any males be generated – around five hundred. But they do not hang around the nest; they do not forage; they do not build. Instead they set off to gather around treetops and prominent bushes to await potential mates.

The dominance of females in every wasp colony goes some way to explaining the lack of much folk knowledge when it comes to the fact that male wasps cannot sting – after all, since male wasps are so scarce it is no surprise that in the past people did not come across them or easily discover their stinglessness. Instead, they found that every wasp nest they blundered into was full to bursting with aggressive stinging females.

Not all females are created equal, however. Aristotle knew that in each wasp nest the 'leader' was bigger and gentler than the vast hordes doing all the work. He also knew that some wasps were stingless, like drones (male honeybees). It's pretty obvious that much of the ancients' biological knowledge of wasps was

Wasp costume design by Attilio Comelli for a production of *Babes in the Wood* at the Drury Lane Theatre, London, 1907. In wing shape, abdominal pattern, antennal form and narrowing waist the anatomical correctness is very pleasing – so we can forgive the wrong number of limbs.

extrapolated from honeybees, and that the three forms of inhabitant in the wasp nest were considered exactly equivalent to those found in domestic beehives. But what were those inhabitants exactly?

There was a lot of room for confusion. When discussing bees and wasps, Aristotle (and plenty of subsequent authors) talks about the 'leader' of the colony, and although this is often in masculine terms (, *basileus*, 'king' and , *igemon*, 'ruler'), he is careful to note that some call this leader the 'good mother' of the hive.[2] Vagueness continued for many centuries. Both Edward Topsell and Thomas Muffet (quoting Conrad Gessner from the sixteenth century) talk of the queens in terms of leaders, chieftains, masters, commanders, captains and princes, all masculine titles at the time. Muffet's 1658 English translation quotes Pliny the Elder, where at the end of the season 'the chieftain or master wasp (which is called the matrix) procreates no more wasps [workers] but those of his own sex'.[3] Despite the identification of the queen as being a he, that archaic word matrix is Latin for 'breeding female animal', later in the sense of 'womb' and comes from *mater* or *matr-* meaning mother. Not that this indicates much understanding because he goes on to suggest that 'all the summer they are governed by their masters or male wasps, but in the winter by their females'.

There was also some debate about whether the good (and gentle) king/queen had a sting. The reticence of the 'leader' in the comb, always unwilling to enter combat, perhaps explains an uncertainly about the queen/king's possession of a weapon. To some extent it might have depended on whether he/she was male or female. Aristotle thought that since nature arms only the male of a species, stinging worker wasps and bees must be males but the unarmed drones must be females. In the *Iliad*, Homer has Asius rushing out from Troy and chafing with vexation that his

Greek (obviously male) enemies will not engage his soldiers when he wants them to, comparing them to wasps guarding their nest. Ever since, the error has been continued such that aggressive wasps and hornets are always described as 'he'. This is quite the reverse of our modern scientific understanding.

There were other considerations when debating the sex of the sting-possessing worker wasps and bees; it was obvious that they were foraging for food and feeding the offspring in the brood combs, but elsewhere in nature males do not tend their young (no one, it seems, had been paying much attention to birds, where males regularly take on these domestic duties). Anyway, it was all very confusing. To a certain extent, Aristotle's meagre biological knowledge of insect gender was overshadowed by a huge ignorance about how bees and wasps bred in the first place. Bees and wasps were never seen to copulate. At the time it was widely held (not by Aristotle though) that bees were spontaneously generated from the fermenting body of an ox that had had its eyes, nose and mouth blocked to prevent the soul escaping. Wasps, it transpired, were likely to be similarly generated from the corpse of a donkey. Both Ovid and Pliny suggested wasps came from a horse carcass, while hornets arose from the body of a war horse, although when their erudite Greek is translated into English it sounds like childish doggerel: 'When war-horse dead upon the earth lies, then doth his flesh breed hornet flies.'[4]

These archaic notions were tied into the origin of the bugonia oxen-born bee myth, first mooted by Nicander of Colophon in the second century BC. In Greek mythology Aristaeus was in big trouble with Eurydice's nymphs; she had trodden on a snake and been bitten and killed as she tried to escape his amorous attentions, so the nymphs killed all his bees. He had to appease them by sacrificing four bulls and four heifers. Nine days of putrefaction later and the insects miraculously spewed out of the dead animals. A millennium and a half later this idea was still being peddled in some quarters, although the Italian scholar, scientist and opposer of the idea of spontaneous generation Francesco Redi (1626–1697) is scornful of the fables that hornets were supposed to be generated by 'the hard parts of horse flesh, and wasps in the tender parts'. Likewise Topsell, paraphrasing Gessner, considered it unlikely that 'Some wasps do proceed from the stinking carcase of a crocodile, if we may give credit to the Egyptians and their followers', and it is fairly obvious that he didn't give them an ounce of credit.[5] In reality these insects were most likely to be honeybee- and wasp-mimicking hoverflies, some of which breed in semi-liquid putrescent carrion. Again, there were nuggets of first-hand knowledge around at the time, but much was hidden or misunderstood, clouded in mystery, hearsay and superstition.

It was not until Charles Butler's *The Feminine Monarchie* (1609) that the true gender of the queen bee (and workers) was proposed. This was later confirmed by microscope dissection of the queen's ovaries by Jan Swammerdam in 1668. The realization that wasp-nest sexual economy worked along the same lines as honeybees' sexual economy did duly fell into place by default. There then followed several reiterated accounts, often alluding to the Amazons, and likening the all-female insect colonies of wasps to the mythical race of warrior women.

There was already a natural, though slightly coincidental, link between wasps and femininity, and whether this was bolstered by a subliminal understanding of wasp gender and colony structure or not, it reached its height (though narrowest point might be more apt) in the nineteenth century. Here wasp-waisted, corset-induced abdominal constriction became the fashion statement of the day. As described earlier, the narrow pedicel of the wasp abdomen gives supple flexibility, allowing the sting-tipped tail to angle in almost any direction. By contrast the fashion victim's whalebone-stiffened corsets restricted movement and breathing and led to weakened abdominal muscles and deformed internal organs, often resulting in miscarriage and maternal death.

This overemphasized narrow Barbie waist continues to haunt modern women. It was obvious to the most novice comic book readers that when Marvel introduced The Wasp it would be a svelte narrow-waisted woman who played the alter-ego alongside the diminutive bravado of Ant-Man. The glamorous sexualized costume designs that went with the character are typical of the genre. It is also pretty obvious that cartoonist Bill Watterson's exuberant six-year-old Calvin and his toy tiger Hobbes were discussing a disguised version of this superhero when Hobbes asks: 'Is Amazon Girl's super power the ability to squeeze that figure into that suit?' 'Nah,' says Calvin, 'they all can do that.'

THE SEX LIVES OF WASPS

One of the reasons that nobody had noted wasps (or bees) mating, was that coitus occurs well away from the colony. Topsell wondered 'if they couple together, they do it by night, as cats do, or else in some secret corner that Argus with his hundred eyes can never espy it'.[6] Male wasps quickly leave the nest on hatching from the chrysalis in the brood comb. They make no contribution to the nest economy and depart immediately. They then take to lounging about on leaves near the top of a prominent bush or tree. Here they gather in large numbers (many hundreds recorded) and wait for virgin queens, also emerging from their pupal brood cells at this time. This sloth had long been known in the wastrel male honeybees, and became perfectly personified by P. G. Wodehouse in the Drones Club where Bertie Wooster and other typically idle rich Edwardian gentlemen of leisure gossiped and drank. Wasp mating remains elusive and secretive. When entomologist

Sir Edward Bagnall Poulton (1856–1943) first observed this behaviour he was so keen not to miss the opportunity to examine them that he captured the wasps in his hat. It took three or four attempts and ended in the busy road: 'This was a risk that I felt must not be repeated and accordingly pressed the hat against my body as soon as the wasps had entered it. Thus safely enclosed they were easily taken back to my house which was near at hand . . . It was evident that coitus at this stage is not to be ended by repeated and very considerable disturbance.'[7] Mating behaviour is seldom seen or understood in wasps and this is reflected in the sad fact that male wasps still do not have their own vernacular name – perhaps, in future, wapstrel might suffice?

Probably attracted to the male aggregations by some communally exuded masculine pheromone scent, the new queen wasps appear and are pounced on by the assembled males. Had it been observed by Aristotle, Pliny, Columella or even medieval writers, this behaviour would not have seemed unusual at all, as it has direct similarities to the familiar world of game birds. In a behaviour called lekking, males of numerous birds, including black grouse and capercaillie, gather together in raucous displays where many dozens of noisy cock birds preen and strut while a small number of hens choose their suitors. Male lekking is widespread among insects, with well-known examples including flies, bumblebees, honeybees and, of course, wasps.

Wasp leks, sometimes coyly called nuptial gatherings, are not often observed, even by experienced naturalists, despite the fact that they occur openly during the middle of the day in full view of Argus with his hundred eyes. This is partly because they are not sought out but also because they happen mostly out of sight at treetop height. Unlike the leisurely intercourse of beetles and butterflies sitting on flowers, wasp sex happens in a trice. A male unceremoniously pounces on a female and grapples her onto a leaf, or to the ground; a brief squirming conjugation grapple and it's done. They may remain together, as Poulton had seen, for some minutes, but often another male (or more) from the lek will interrupt and break up the pair. It is perhaps no wonder that ancient Greek and Roman writers did not quite know what was going on. If it is almost forgivable that wasp mating was not properly observed by early natural philosophers, what happened next was a complete mystery that only close observation and modern microscopy would solve – how does a colony produce three, instead of the usual two, genders? The secrets of wasp sex remain obscure, but by inference, they must follow those of the closely related but much better studied honeybee.

Once it was confirmed that queens and worker wasps were all female, and that the stingless males were produced, along with new queens, in small numbers at the end of the year, some sort of biological explanation was deemed necessary. First, how could wasps control the sex of their offspring to produce only female workers during the early part of the year, but both females and males when required later? It was a Polish bee-keeper, Johann Dzierzon, who first suggested in 1845 that a mated queen bee (and by analogy a queen wasp) could lay two types of egg: eggs fertilized with sperm, which developed into females, and unfertilized eggs which became males.[8] This is the basis of the complex biological marvel called haplodiploid sex determination.

In the standard body cell of a typical organism the genetic material of the DNA is gathered into discrete accumulations – the chromosomes – visible down the high-power microscope at certain points of the cell division cycle when they were appropriately stained with chemical reagents. Different genes, for different bodily characteristics, are grouped and carried on particular individual chromosomes, which can also be differentiated down the microscope eyepiece by their varied sizes and stain-colouring patterns. Throughout almost all living plants, animals and fungi, the chromosomes are paired – 23 pairs in humans, three pairs in the yellow fever mosquito, sixteen pairs in honeybees, eighteen pairs in carrots, 308 pairs in black mulberry and 25 pairs in the common wasp *Vespula vulgaris*. As an organism grows its cells divide and multiply within its body and the chromosomes multiply and divide too – first doubling in number, then splitting apart into two daughter cells, maintaining that full complement of pairs (the diploid condition) throughout almost every cell in the body. The only exceptions are in the sex cells – eggs and sperm – when the pairs become separated and only one of each chromosome is contained within; this is a haploid condition. Thus, at the point of fertilization (conception) an egg and a sperm unite to re-establish the fully paired diploid cohort of chromosomes. Except something different happens in wasps and bees.

Hornets, *Vespa crabro*: not a mating pair since the upper specimen is a worker, but the photo does show the slightly longer down-curved antennae of the male.

During mating, the male delivers sperm to the female queen – this much is common across all animals – but egg/sperm union does not take place immediately. Instead, the female wasp stores the sperm for future use in a reservoir in her abdomen, the sperm-atheca, and keeps it safe for weeks or months until she needs it. Only at the point of egg laying does the female wasp decide to fertilize (or not) an egg with sperm. If this happens, the haploid egg (25 single chromosomes) and sperm (also 25 single chromosomes) combine to create a diploid embryo with fifty chromosomes – those full 25 pairs. This will develop into a female wasp. If, on the other hand, the egg is not fertilized with sperm it remains haploid, with only the 25 maternal chromosomes, and this will develop into a male wasp. This counter-intuitive mechanism determines maleness or femaleness across all wasps, bees and ants, indeed across the entire diversity of the Hymenoptera, and also occurs sporadically across a few groups of beetles, thrips, spider mites and rotifers. It is odd, very odd indeed, but it works, and it later explains some of the mysteries of colony and population dynamics.

There is obviously enough sperm to go round, because the vast majority of social wasps are female workers. This does tend to confound anyone portraying wasps in stories, where a natural anthropomorphic response is to offer them up as a more familiar male/female mix. When some renegade ants in the 1998 Dream-Works film *Antz* come across two wasps buzzing about a picnic, the pair are portrayed as man and wife, a wild departure from any real scenario. Mind you, the worker ants in the film are all macho males (like wasps they should be females), a scientific fault line that bends credulity for any entomologist watching.

Quite how or why a female wasp decides, or not, to add sperm to the egg passing down her egg-laying duct is still a bit of a mystery. But breeding experiments, mostly in honeybees, using slightly differently coloured races clearly show that the body coloration of the male is passed onto his daughters (the workers and queens, who acquire his DNA through the act of fertilization), but does not appear in the nest's sons, which get their chromo-somal DNA only from their mother. In a human society dominated by patriarchy and firstborn male heir inheritance norms, female-controlled haplodiploidy remains a widely ignored and suspicious notion. It must surely be a powerful theme for a science fiction story – one that was only partly touched on in James Cameron's *Aliens* (1986), sequel to the iconic 1979 Ridley Scott production *Alien*. At the end of the film the bloated insectoid alien queen is seen laying thousands of eggs in a deep subterranean cavern. Maybe there's room for the drone of the species in yet another sequel – *Malien*?

WORKERS? LET THEM EAT . . . WHATEVER THEY'RE GIVEN

The next conceptual problem to overcome was the question of why some wasp females go on to become fully sexually mature queens (also called gynes in the technical literature), whilst the majority of the sisters remain drudge workers? It all seems to be down to nutrition. Yet again, the process is better understood in domesticated honeybees, where protein-rich secretions from inside the throats of the workers provide a top-quality nutritional start to a maggot's life. After a few days the bee larvae are weaned off it and start to receive protein from collected pollen and carbo-hydrate from nectar or stored honey. Future queens, on the other hand, continue to receive the throat secretions, so much so that globs of it accumulate in their larger-than-average comb cells and it is often referred to as royal jelly. By virtue of their better nutritional intake as larvae they become larger and their ovaries mature, ready for mating and reproduction. Workers, though, remain small and stunted; often referred to as neuters in some older textbooks, some are able to lay eggs, but since workers do not (or cannot) mate, their eggs remain unfertilized and are therefore destined to become haploid males – that is, if their eggs are allowed to develop, which most are not since they are cleaned out of the brood cells by other jealous workers.

Queen or worker development in wasps is not so well understood, but also seems linked to food quality. Unlike bees, wasp larvae all receive 100 per cent protein-rich chewed insect remains from their forager worker sisters. Experimental interference with feeding regimes, thus counteracting any worker-inducing food deprivation, produces bigger and heavier workers, but does not prompt more queen production; it must be some subtle chemical or hormonal effect on their development. No royal-jelly-like secretions have so far been observed in wasps, but this hasn't stopped the usual confused science fiction speculation. In *The Wasp Woman*, released in 1959 during the heyday of giant insect/horror/mutant/half-human B-movies, a rogue cosmetics scientist distils anti-ageing enzymes from 'queen wasp jelly' with predictable, hilarious half-insect side effects.

Without any royal jelly, the quality of food given to putative queen wasp larvae nevertheless appears to be higher in its nitrogen content than that given to grubs destined to become mere workers. Gonad production, it turns out, is hugely nitrogen-expensive. It's not that the foragers test the nutritional nitrogen in each morsel they serve up to the larvae, more that herbivore prey items (moths, butterflies, their plant-eating caterpillars, bees, leaf-hoppers), are less rich in nitrogen than predator prey further up the food chain – things like hoverflies with aphid-eating larvae, other wasps, or carrion-feeding blowflies.[9] It is tantalizing to imagine that the wasp foragers can somehow taste the difference between a herbivore and a carnivore insect, much the way that most human meat-eating is based on the more subtle

Unlikely wasp/woman chimera – publicity material for the slightly laughable black-and-white science-fiction horror film *The Wasp Woman* (1959).

A BEAUTIFUL WOMAN BY DAY–
A LUSTING QUEEN WASP BY NIGHT.
The WASP WOMAN
STARRING
SUSAN CABOT · FRED EISLEY · BARBOURA MORRIS
Produced and Directed by ROGER CORMAN · Written by LEO GORDON

taste of plant-fed farm animals, rather than the rank, sometimes over-fragrant flesh of dog or cat, fox or ferret.

An adult wasp does not live very long. At the height of midsummer activity, workers are exhausted and perish at anything from 4 to 28 days – they are quite literally worked to death. Even during the relative calm of that milk and honey time in August, when prey is plentiful and construction work on the nest has ebbed, the span is barely increased to ten to forty days.[10] Males don't have it much easier – with nowhere to live or shelter (they are ejected from the nest in which they were raised) and with no biological purpose other than to mate with a queen, most males die after copulating. Only queens, sustained by a superior body-build based on their high larval nitrogen intake, live any meaningful time, but few survive longer than twelve months.

After a newly hatched virgin queen has mated, her first act is to find somewhere safe and dry to overwinter – under a piece of loose bark, inside a hollow tree trunk or behind the curtains of the spare room. The queen clamps down hard with her clawed legs, draws her furled wings underneath her body, adopts a stiff hunched pose and turns down her metabolism to bare tick-over. Here she remains in hibernation torpor until the following spring. It may have been the discovery of these inactive, thoroughly non-aggressive and easy to handle hibernating queens that gave rise to the widely held folk belief that wasps shed their stings in winter. If they wake indoors though, disturbed prematurely by the turning up of the central heating, queen wasps are very likely to be trodden on in bare feet, with the usual painful consequences.

In one of the few poems in English about vespids, 'Upon a wasp chilled with cold', Edward Taylor (c. 1644–1729) could be

A widowed winter-survivor

describing a queen rousing slowly from her winter slumber: 'whose stiffened limbs encramped, lay bathing, in Sol's warm breath . . . her hands she chafes and stands, rubbing her legs, shanks, thighs and hands. Her pretty toes and fingers' ends . . . she out extends unto the sun in great desire, to warm her digits in that fire.' Wasps groom themselves with their legs, running their middle and back legs over their abdomen and wings, smoothing their antennae through a special spurred groove on their front legs. Wasps don't have pretty toes and fingers, but Taylor's words are well-suited to the awakening queen's delicate movements before 'she fans her wing up to the wind, as if her petticoat were lined, with reason's fleece' and she sets off into the air, 'hoists sails, and humming flies in thankful gales'. It turns out that this Puritan poet

Two hibernating queens sheltering under loose bark, their wings drawn in tight underneath their bodies to avoid damage, condensation and fungal attack. Mortality at this stage is high, with wasps vulnerable to moulds, mice and spiders, next to whose webs these wasps are roosting.

was probably alluding to a much more sensuous arousal, with the wasp actually being a metaphor for the beautiful woman his religious sensibilities prevented him from writing about directly, but the description well fits wasp behaviour in springtime.[11]

Depending on the wasp species and the precise orientation of the overwintering site to the slanting rays of the sun, queens emerge any time from mid-March to mid-May. Each then sets about founding a new nest and she must toil alone to get things going.

ROYAL PURGATORY

During her year of life the queen spends most of her time laying something in the order of 15,000 eggs, most of which will be fertilized with that stored sperm, and which will grow to become females. The first fifteen or so are laid in cells of the small embryo nest she creates – about the size of a golf ball, and these will be the first cohort of nutritionally deprived, neutered workers. She catches insect prey and feeds the chewed gloop to the grubs, which spend about ten days feeding and growing. When they are fully grown, the maggots weave a pale silken cap to cover the cell. They spend the next ten days making the magical metamorphic transmogrification into an adult wasp and soon join the queen to take over hunting, nest-building, comb-cleaning and colony-protecting duties.

The queen is not off the hook though. Rather than the life of leisure her royal name might suggest, she simply becomes the egg factory for the nest. A cell vacated by a newly emerged worker is empty for just a day or so before another egg takes up residence and the process continues remorselessly.

Far from a life of royal privilege, the queen is more or less a prisoner in her own nest. She becomes faded and blotchy; the bright colours of her youth become greasy and dull. The soft down of fine hairs that once covered her handsome body wears away until she is bald. Her delicate wingtips become ragged and torn, probably through constant scratching from her workers' claws as they clamber over her. She is at least spared the very real dangers faced by her worker daughters – predators, getting lost, inundation from the rain.

She is also well nourished, but in a perverse reversal of what might be considered normal adult behaviour, she is actually fed by her own offspring. Wasp maggots do not defecate. Each sitting in a cul-de-sac paper cell, they would soon be mired in their own excrement if they passed their waste in the conventional way. Instead, they digest their protein-rich chewed-insect meals and incorporate almost all of it into their own body structure. It is carbohydrate sugars that they have in excess, and these they regurgitate as a droplet whenever an adult wasp passes. The fluid also contains other pre-digested nutrients like amino acids. The wasps gulp down this sweet liquor, a veritable power-packed soup, and it is this alone which sustains the comb-bound queen.

During late summer the queen starts to lay unfertilized eggs, which will develop into haploid males, but she has not run out of stored sperm since conventional female eggs also continue to be laid, and some of these are now destined to become new nutritionally favoured queens. As the season closes, the old queen will eventually run out of steam and die, but the new queens will emerge, mate and find new overwintering spots to begin the process anew next year.

4 Paper Architecture

The most wonderful of wasp behaviours is, without doubt, their nest construction. In his stirring praise poem 'Jubilate Agno' (Rejoice in the Lamb, 1759–63), poet and scholar Christopher Smart is chiefly remembered for celebrating his cat Jeoffry, his lone companion while confined for lunacy in St Luke's Hospital, Bethnal Green. However the first portion of this epic work, where he pairs Old Testament patriarchs with various animals, he says, 'Let Zorobabel bless with the wasp, who is the Lord's architect, and buildeth his edifice in armour'.[1] Zorobabel (or Zerubbabel) built a temple in Jerusalem and is mentioned in some branches of freemasonry. Although he was writing a treatise on honeybees, Thomas Wildman mentions wasps in passing: 'we judge thus ill of them only for want of knowing them . . . The republics of wasps are in nothing inferior to those of bees.'[2] Having said that, his Book 3, on wasps and hornets, was primarily concerned with killing them, and this usually meant finding and destroying those architecturally celebrated nests using gunpowder and cyanide.

In non-social species (usually called solitary wasps, for their lonely working lives) a single female insect toils alone to make a simple burrow in the soil or she may use a hollow plant stem, or a tunnel already dug by a beetle in a dead tree trunk. This she stocks with dead insects – flies, caterpillars, spiders, whatever her palate and specialist hunting tactics can provide, and in which

Plate from Audubon's *Birds of America* (1838), showing a paper wasp nest, probably *Polistes fuscatus* – very likely prey for the American redstart *Muscicapa* (now *Setophaga*) *ruticilla*. Once found, it will be visited many times as the wasps are picked off individually and taken to be fed to the young birds back in the nest.

she lays her eggs. The grubs hatch and feed on the stored food, but they have no contact with their mother wasp, and she will be long dead when they emerge from the burrow as adults next spring. But the social wasps – they build bustling cities of paper.

The simplest nests are small parabolic umbrella-shaped constructions, attached to a twig or under a stone outcrop, hanging from a single slender stalk. These are constructed by the so-called paper wasps, *Polistes* and the like. This is a bit of a misnomer because all social wasps use paper to make their nests, so umbrella wasps would be a much better name. Cells are built on the underside of the umbrella, rarely numbering more than two hundred, and with colony numbers of usually only a few scores.

The nests are dainty and fragile, easily knocked (giving the wasps a bit of a reputation, but also easily moved. British politician and naturalist Sir John Lubbock kept a pet *Polistes* queen.

Nest of the African paper wasp *Belonogaster juncea*, marking an intermediate stage in sociality; though there are no sterile workers, daughters stay with their mothers and do most of the foraging and nest construction, while older females devote themselves to egg-laying.

> I took her, with her nest, in the Pyrenees, early in May . . .
> I had no difficulty in inducing her to feed on my hand; but at first she was shy and nervous. She kept her sting in readiness; and once or twice in the train, when the railway officials came for tickets, and I was compelled to hurry her back into her bottle, she stung me slightly – I think, however, entirely from fright.[3]

Nest of *Polistes dominulus* from Thames Barrier Park, London, September 2007 – the first time this mainly European wasp was found breeding out of doors in the British Isles. It had previously been found nesting inside the roof of the orangery of Ham House, Richmond.

Plate from a Victorian entomology textbook showing the diversity and artistry of various wasp nests. Whether by author or editorial error, the plate appears to be upside down: almost all of these small nests are usually constructed open-cell-end down, to avoid being flooded when it rains; they were probably engraved from removed museum specimens.

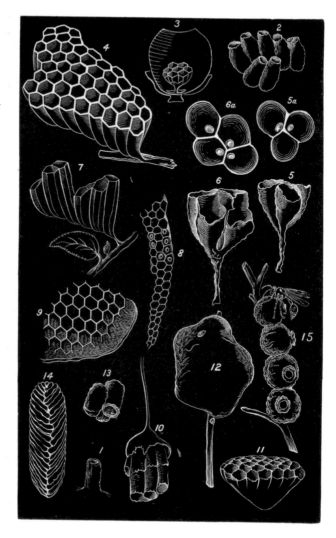

Nests of *Chartergus* and *Myrapetra* (now *Polybius*) wasps; these take various splendid architectural forms and were perfect to demonstrate the wonder of creation in *Romance of the Insect World* (1893).

She lived in his Kent home for several months and when she died he was moved to eulogize: 'She could but wag her tail, a last token of gratitude and affection.'[4] He then donated her body to the Natural History Museum where she resides still, pinned in the Hymenoptera collections there.

The umbrella-shaped nests of umbrella wasps are pretty and decorative and range from simple mushroom domes to slender

Illustration from 1768 showing that wasp nests come in many shapes and sizes. These were obviously drawn from museum specimens as the undissected nest at bottom left should have its entrance hole beneath, not to the side; and the small cut-away embryo nest is upside down.

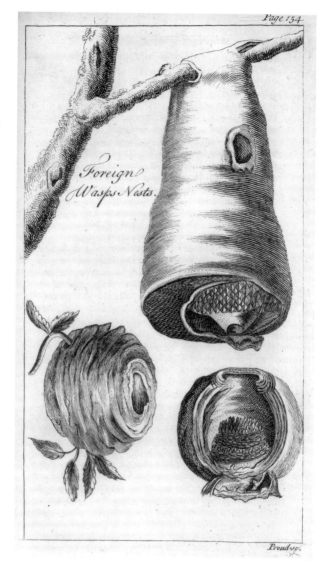

Page 154.

Foreign Wasps Nests.

Proud sc.

feather-shaped arches, but they pale in comparison to the vast metropolises of the true vespines. These are the astounding sculptural teardrop- or beachball-shaped structures often found in lofts to the consternation of concerned residents. Edward Topsell writing in 1658 was full of praise for the many nest shapes that he claimed he had personally witnessed: 'Their nests or houses are not all made after one fashion, but very different, some of them presenting a harp, some made much after the fashion of a pear, a toadstool, a bottle or budget [flask] of leather, and some like a standing cup with handles.'[5]

The outer, gently contoured protective carton is an organic and flowing shape that could be the gnarled excrescence of a large

Active hornet nest inside a hollow tree trunk. The distinctively overlapping scales of the nest are clearly shown.

tree trunk, or the hardened nodule of some subterranean lava flow, but the brood combs within are a marvel of engineering, the repeated hexagonal patterns contrasting spectacularly against their amorphous shell. It is easy to tell if a wasp nest is still occupied – the whole construction acts like a hi-fi speaker and amplifies the buzzing of the wasps inside. There is an Egyptian proverb: 'the buzzing of the wasp brought ruin to its nest'; this is the equivalent of 'he had it coming to him', but is possibly rooted in the ability to tell whether the nest is still active before its ruin is brought about by anxious homeowners.

The entire nest is constructed of paper, which the wasps make by chewing wood fibres from dead or living trees, logs, stumps, fence posts, exposed house timbers or indeed discarded newspaper. Oddly, Aristotle was unsure what the nest material was; he described it as bark-like, with something of the cobweb about it, and wondered if wood chippings, shavings or soil were incorporated. It was a good guess. The Incredible String Band made a useful description when they sang of 10,000 brothers in a nest of fungus paper; someone should have pointed out that they were sisters though.

Common wasp, *Vespula vulgaris*, chewing wood fibres from a fence post. The pale rasp marks made by the sharp jaws cutting across the grain of the wood are clearly visible.

Close-up of wasp nest carton showing individual lines of wood pulp laid down by individual worker wasps. This is an old, disused nest from a loft and is already starting to break up and collapse.

Landing parallel to the grain of the wood, the wasp gnaws the surface, leaving distinct irregular abraded ribbon patches. The rasping of a wasp's jaws against the wood is clearly audible to a close observer. Eventually, after one to four minutes, a small ball of fibres, chewed and mixed with saliva, is gathered under the head, between the front legs. When it is about 3 mm across the ball weighing 1.2–2.8 mg is carried in the legs, back to the nest site.[6] Here it is chewed and mixed with more saliva, then spread and shaped by the jaws. The outer cartons of most wasp nests, appearing like a series of overlapping scalloped scales, are prettily marked with minute undulating lines of lighter and darker paper, showing where each individual wasp builder has deposited its chewed load of wood pulp. The frequently paler, yellowish nests of *Vespula vulgaris* are produced by extensive use of well-rotted wood, where the greyer nests of *Vespula germanica* display sounder fibres, though there is huge variability and flexibility.

Wasps will use whatever building materials they can find and under experimental conditions they can be induced to build

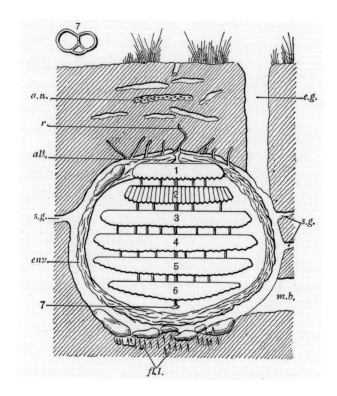

Cross-section of *Vespula germanica* nest, from the Victorian encyclopaedia *The Natural History of Animals*. This is slightly stylized; in truth no wasp nest is quite so exactly regimented but instead grows in a flowing, organic form as it is gradually enlarged.

multi-coloured psychedelic nests from offered coloured paper. Reverend J. G. Wood tells of a nest constructed entirely from the blue-and-white cartridge casings thrown away by soldiers.[7] In the science-fantasy short story 'The Cartographer Wasps and the Anarchist Bees' by E. Lily Yu, residents of the Chinese village of Yiwei discover that the wasp nests in their neighbourhood, doused with boiling water, unfurl to reveal 'beautifully accurate maps of provinces near and far, inked in vegetable pigments and labeled in careful Mandarin that could be distinguished beneath a microscope'.[8] Whether through fear or curiosity the villagers decimate the local wasp population until the remaining handful, 'commanded by a single stubborn foundress' (right sex, good), fold a paper boat to float away down the river in search of new lands. The story turns into a metaphor for colonization and empire as the wasps conquer the local bees, and exact by threat a levy in honey and grubs, but the notion of scholarly artistic geometer scribes inside the paper tracery of the nest is a nice turn against the usual representation of wasps as mere stinging barbarians.

Unlike honeybees, which can maintain their nest year on year (potentially for ever), each wasp nest is started fresh in spring, and begins with a single queen, emerging from hibernation, working on her own. She chews her own wood pulp and dangles a small umbrella dome from a stalk-like attachment; she extends this into a ¾ globe about the size of a golf ball and underneath she begins her embryo nest with about fifteen hexagonal cells. Inside each cell she glues an egg, and when the eggs hatch into grubs she has to forage and feed them. At night, and if the weather is inclement,

Engraving of dissected embryo nest, Shaw and Nodder, *The Naturalist's Miscellany* (1810).

87

she huddles around the precursor comb and uses her own body heat to keep the nest at an ideal 18–22 degrees celsius.[9] This is a dangerous time, with an estimated nine successful new colonies established from ten thousand hibernating queens. In other words, there is a 99.9 per cent mortality rate.

The first cohort of workers, nine or ten of them, set about helping the queen with prey-catching, pulp-chewing and architectural expansion. With a generation time of 23–29 days, the colony can expand exponentially, and there are soon hundreds, then thousands of workers coming and going. The initial golf-ball-sized carton is dismantled and a larger envelope is constructed in layers to house the new brood combs that are constructed in parallel storeys.

The hexagonal cells, like those of the honeybee combs, are a mystery and a wonder to behold. It is still not clear how the beautifully regular symmetry is maintained. In 1658 Thomas Muffet rather supernaturally attributed 'six-square cells according to the number of their feet'.[10] During cell construction there is much testing and manoeuvring around the working surfaces being sculpted; no feet are involved in the manipulation of the papier-mâché, only the jaws. It seems likely that the wasps are using their antennae to measure distances and align the walls into the complex and regular arrays, but in experiments with hornets where one of their antennae has been removed, they are still able to create the mathematically pure hexagons.[11]

There are some key differences between honeybee combs and wasp combs. The first is that wasp combs, like their encompassing cartons, are made entirely of chewed wood-pulp paper. This light, tough, flexible material is perfect to house the wasp grubs; although it is not recycled back into pulp, each cell can be reused several times over the course of the colony's life. Honeybee combs are made of wax, a fatty secretion exuded by special glands on the

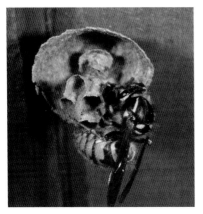

Construction of the embryo nest. The queen works alone to create the first few cells; these become enclosed in a golf-ball-sized carton, and eventually the brood metamorphose into the first cohort of workers.

underside of the worker bees' abdomens. Wax is heavy, but it is long lasting, constantly recyclable and waterproof, so it can contain the honey stores without leaking or becoming sodden.

The brood combs of a wasp nest are ranged horizontally, buttressed together like the floors of a tower block by small pillars

Attempt to show the differences between wasps and bees in an early popular book on insects (1768). The anatomy is not very clear, and the author shows two sorts of female wasp along with the male and worker; the hexagonal back-to-back construction of the bees' honeycomb is nevertheless well depicted.

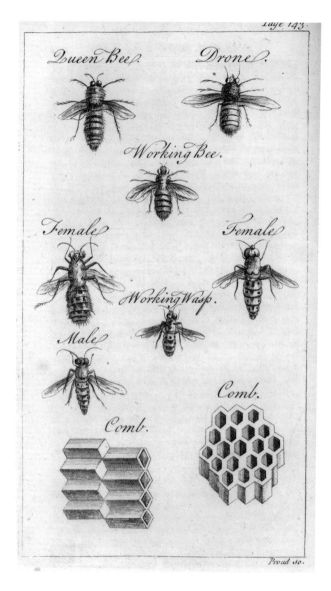

or narrow walls of supportive connecting strips. The cells, with the maggots inside, open downwards. Honeycombs, on the other hand, hang vertically and have a double, back-to-back arrangement of outwardly opening cells. Honey is stiff, but still a liquid, and a bit runny; it can sit happily in the horizontally aligned cells, but would just drip out if the honeycomb cells faced downwards.

The open face of wasp brood cells shows a perfectly neat hexagonal array, but the cells are actually slightly inwardly curved, becoming more circular in cross-section towards the base. This splaying curvature noticeably increases towards the outer edge of each comb. Honeybee cells, with the double layers backing onto each other, are more formally regimented, and more regular in shape and cross section.

SUPER NESTS

As the paper brood combs increase in size and number, the paper carton is adjusted and rebuilt to accommodate them. A dozen combs, roughly 15–20 cm (6–8 in.) across and totalling about 8,000 cells, commonly form a nest the size of a beachball. If the nest is underground (usually *Vespula* species), the small cavern in which the nest sits has to be excavated jawful by jawful by the workers, but inside the void of a loft or attic space the wasps can concentrate on expansion and a large casing the size of an inflated bin bag can result.

Different wasp species naturally produce different-sized nests, often in different situations. The genus *Dolichovespula* makes aerial nests, where the exposed carton, about the size of a honeydew melon, is suspended from a tree branch, or constructed across the tangle of twigs deep in a bush, and rarely contains more than four hundred cells. There is some evidence that aerial nesting is better suited to warm sunny situations; even if sheltered by the

surrounding foliage of the tree or bush the nest is more likely to be affected by daily temperature changes, particularly early in the year when the nest is being built.

Hornets, nesting inside hollow tree trunks and branches, may only have 150 cells, though they are larger, averaging 7.4 mm (0.3 in.) in diameter compared to 4.3 mm (0.17 in.) for *Vespula* cells. They are protected from much of the weather by their enclosed situation, but this has not stopped them entering weather-lore rhymery: 'If hornets build low, winter storm and snow; if hornets build high, winter mild and dry.' Nonsense, of course, but, like all doggerel, good fun.

At the end of the season, after the new males and sexually active gyne queens have departed, the nest soon empties. The last few lingering workers die or dissipate. Soon the shell, no matter how large, is silent and forlorn. A wasp nest is a transient and ephemeral structure, striking enough when it is fully occupied, but soon disappearing to nothing. It must have been a unique quirk of timing that led to one such colony being immortalized in the naming of Wasp Nest Road in Huddersfield, Yorkshire. Usually a carton nest will never be used again. Unless they occur in New Zealand.

The Antipodes have no native vespine wasps, but *Vespula germanica* was accidentally introduced into New Zealand in 1945, *Vespula vulgaris* in 1978 (singletons had previously been turning up since 1922 and 1921 respectively, but colonies had never become established).[12] They probably arrived as lone hibernating queens tucked away in packaging materials used to transport goods, having gained access in the cool autumnal calm of a British warehouse, and roused a few weeks later in the balmy southern hemisphere. Having discovered a blank canvas land in which there was no similar competition, both species spread wildly and soon became notorious pests. An early eradication attempt which involved collecting hibernating queens (and offering a bounty) failed, even though 118,000 queens were collected and destroyed, including 7,000 by one schoolboy.

Something odd now happened in the warm subtropical mountainsides of the Waitakere Ranges, in the North Island, just west of Auckland. Instead of the normal colony decline as the season moved into autumn, the nests continued to grow, lasting several years, often with multiple closely related sister queens (sometimes hundreds) sharing egg-laying duties. Rather than making subterranean nests, as they do in Europe, both *Vespula* species started to make semi-arboreal nests, beginning in a tree hole like hornets, but then extending and expanding out to envelop the trunk. A nest found in 1952 measured 4.5 m (15 ft) high, 1.5 m (5 ft) wide and 0.6 m (2 ft) thick – about the size of a family saloon car – and contained an estimated 3 to 4 million cells in 180 combs, weighing nearly half a tonne, with probably 400,000 workers active at any time.[13] This was truly a monster, and a significant

Giant *Vespula germanica* nest in New Zealand, 1952.

threat to the health of local people and wildlife. A similar lack of senescence sometimes also occurs in subtropical California and Florida, where the equally invasive European wasp species can produce two- or three-year nests the size of a fridge-freezer. But most reports of 'giant' wasp nests are mere exaggeration, simply because the impressive nests discovered in abandoned sheds or seldom-visited loft spaces seem incomprehensibly large given the small size of the occupants. The super nests in New Zealand remain unusual, but show how once-familiar cycles of colony growth and demise can be usurped if superimposed on a new environment with new and different seasonal conditions.

If anything the giant New Zealand nests are even more worrying than the nests of giant wasps with which H. G. Wells populated his *Food of the Gods and How it Came to Earth*. In this novel, giant wasps, 70 centimetres (27.5 in.) across the wings, which terrorized the Kent Weald from Westerham to Tonbridge, had managed to feed on a special nutritional superdrug heroically named Herakleophorbia IV, concocted in the laboratory; then they escaped. It took both barrels of a shotgun to bring down a flying wasp, which coincidentally were very similar in size to the giant wasps as big as partridges that assailed Jonathan Swift's hapless traveller Gulliver in Brobdingnag. However, once the nest hole was blocked with great masses of plaster of Paris, it could be destroyed by the traditional application of burning sulphur and nitre – tonnes of the stuff.

THE MYTH OF THE WASP SWARM

If one wasp sting is bad, then multiple stings must be an act of warfare. However, wasps are not the disciplined army of braying Amazons they are sometimes alleged to be. Those reports of life-threatening mass stingings are horrendous, but so rare as to be easily misconstrued. The main danger is stepping into a subterranean nest, breaking through the thin covering of soil, and crushing the combs to arouse the angry occupants, half of which will already be stuffed up a trouser leg. This is not the image most often portrayed though.

Typically, at its stereotypical worst, a cartoon wasp nest is usually depicted as one of the aerial cartons, hanging from the branch of a tree in a most unlikely exposed situation. Given a knock from a passing comedy plank of wood, ladder or clumsy tall person, or following a direct hit from Dennis the Menace's catapult, the wasps stream out and pursue the hapless victim in an ominous angry thundercloud. This is hyperbole gone too far. Sure enough, wasps busy inside the damaged nest pile out to see what is going on, but they are less than coordinated. They don't need to be when it is easy for each of them to see a great hulking silhouette hovering right over the nest entrance. Be this bear, badger or bumbling gardener, the wasps move in to attack an obvious target, but they are not under synchronized orders from some central controlling intelligence – that's bees. As usual, too much half-understood honeybee lore is being mashed up here. Honeybee swarming is a natural part of colony division, when a queen leaves the existing colony with a large cohort of workers to found a new nest elsewhere. Great clouds of many thousands of bees filling the air can be quite unnerving, but when they come to rest in a great heaving mass the size of a football they are remarkably docile and can be easily and safely manipulated by the bee-keeper into a new skep or hive box. This is, traditionally, how keepers increased the numbers of their hives. On the other hand, wasps do not swarm – not to nest, not to break away to a new colony and not to attack. Even Aristotle knew this.

If anything, attacks from wasps are much less worrying than those from honeybees. When a honeybee stings a human, the sting shaft complete with pulsating venom sac is ripped from its abdomen and remains hooked into the skin. The pain continues because the poison is still being injected, even though the disembowelled bee has been knocked off. At the same time a volatile alarm pheromone scent released from the still-pumping venom reservoir fills the air and excites and alerts other members of the hive. They will actively pursue their perceived attacker, who is now labelled with a chemical tag as 'the enemy'. More honeybee workers are drawn to this tag to get their own stings ripped out and more danger signal volatiles are released into the melee. Honeybees can be extremely dangerous because of this escalating attack response.

Wasp stings also release a warning alarm pheromone to recruit other warriors to nest defence, but because the wasp sting lancets are not so barbed and don't get stuck in human skin, the victim is not so easily flagged up as the foe to be followed. The alarm is also not so great as in honeybees – only wasp workers inside the nest are alerted; foragers returning from their travels ignore it. The usual advice to avoid repeat wasp stings is to move away quickly from the nest; this is not just to get you out of sight of the defending wasps (although they do have relatively good vision), but to get you as far from their chemoreceptor scent-sensitive antennae as possible.

Incidentally, the idea of a stereotypical hanging-carton wasp nest also crops up far too often in completely inappropriate situations. From the Middle Ages to the advent of modern printing media, ink was made from what were often reported as wasp nests. However, these were never the large paper nests we're discussing here, or even the small umbrella nests made by *Polistes*. The black-brown ink was made by combining iron (an old nail works) with tannins released from ground-up marble or oak-apple galls made by tiny gall 'wasps' on the buds of oak branches. These are hardly 'nests' by any modern understanding, just wart-like growths resulting from the insects' chemical secretions, but they were quite innocently described as such by earlier writers. They didn't really understand the physiology of the plant's reaction, but knew there was some sort of insect grub (sometimes many) living inside. Unfortunately several modern popular books now wrongly delight in trying to understand the recipes, making ill-founded comments all the while about rampaging stinging insects defending their home. A similar slew of nonsense pictures and text accompanied recent newspaper reports of a bizarre, irresponsible (and possibly dangerous) craze for using a paste made from the ground-up galls to tighten vaginal muscle walls.

IT'S WORTH DEFENDING

Having a sting weapon is not just about personal protection, or even personal hunting; it's about defending the nest. The almost suicidal ferocity with which bees and wasps defend their colonies troubled Charles Darwin and many of the other early evolutionists. They could not explain how the behavioural trait for nest defence at personal cost of death could possibly be passed to the next generation by sterile workers whose only reason for existence was to service the nest. The evolution of altruism by natural selection is still one of the ticklish knots of population biology. It was only with the discovery of haplodiploidy that an understanding came about of the precise genetic equations that mathematically justified the bees' and wasps' actions.

Briefly, it is all about passing genes onto the next generation. Workers get half of their DNA from their father but, because of the haploid nature of the male, they get his entire genome of 25 chromosomes, unaltered, not subject to the usual halving or mixing of chromosome pairs seen in most other animals. This means that rather than full sisters sharing an average of 50 per cent of their DNA with each other, they share 75 per cent. This is also more than the 50 per cent genetic relatedness a conventional non-haplodiploid organism would have with any sons or daughters. Feed these figures into the mathematical models of fecundity, survival rates and genetic flow, and sure enough it is more advantageous for the worker genes' progression into future generations to help the mother produce more queens and males than it is to branch out and start a new family on their own. This was succinctly summed up by biologist and mathematician J.B.S. Haldane (1892–1964). When asked if he would lay down his life for his brother he supposedly replied: 'Two brothers, or eight cousins.'[14]

Defending the nest thus becomes of paramount importance, more important than an individual worker's own life – especially

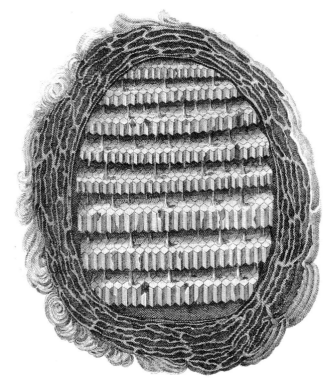

Engraving of a dissected wasp nest showing how the combs are supported by connecting pillars. Shaw and Nodder, *The Naturalist's Miscellany* (1810).

as the nest is constantly under attack, particularly from humans. Its mere presence is usually enough to get householders racing to the telephone to call in the pest-control company to have it removed.

It is not just humans, anxious about being stung, that want to dig up or remove nests. Wasp colonies are also an important source of protein for hungry animals, in the multitudinous soft, easily digestible grubs – thousands of them. In Yorkshire, the combs are sometimes known as wasp cake,[15] but this has more to do with the soft spongy appearance than any palatable piquancy. In many old French books the combs are also referred to as gateaux, with reference to the layering so beloved of patissiers. Vincent Holt's famous little book *Why Not Eat Insects?* may have been intended as slightly tongue-in-cheek scandalous when he suggested wasp grubs baked in the comb, but it turns out that plenty of adventurous people have experimented with this particular dish.[16] Animals are less squeamish than humans, and are happy to have the meal uncooked and ungarnished. The usual culprits are badgers which, with their dense shaving-brush fur, are well protected from the

Vespula germanica workers guard the entrance to their subterranean nest while constantly checking its integrity, enlarging, decreasing or repairing it with their mud-daubing jaws.

Epipona tatua nest. Throughout the world many different wasp species make pendulous aerial nests, hanging from branches.

annoyed guard wasps. In the ongoing ancient muddle between bees and wasps, it is no surprise that two of the best-known but least understood wasp enemies are the Afro-Asian honey badger (the ratel) and the Afro-European honey buzzard; although they will certainly raid feral honeybee nests if they can find them, both predominantly seek out the tasty wasp or hornet brood.

Other frequent wasp-brood predators include moles, house mice and wood mice. Throughout the world bears are also major wasp-nest predators. But again wasp/bee mix-ups and the notion that they are really after honey has displaced any genuine folk knowledge of their true appetites. Winnie-the-Pooh has many adventures after honey, including trying to raid a bumblebees' nest high in a tree. Honeybees sometimes establish wild colonies

The ratel, or honey badger, from Thomas Bewick's *A General History of Quadrupeds* (originally published in 1790). Although his text speaks of 'secret retreats where the bees deposit their stores', wasp nests are their primary food source, and the detail in this illustration looks more like wasp-brood paper-comb than wax honeycomb.

in hollow trunks, but this is much more likely a hornet nesting site. Yogi Bear had a particularly soft spot for honey, usually located in a nest in a hollow log (again, much more likely to house hornets) and involving at least one sting in the backside. Rudyard Kipling does not mention bees or wasps in his original *Jungle Book*, but the 2016 live-action remake of the Disney version features Baloo the sloth bear cajoling Mowgli into helping him get some honey-comb from a cliff overhang. It is quite likely that sometimes, very occasionally, bears might eat honey, but it's wasps they normally go for. This is why wasps have evolved such effective stinging weapons – to defend their homes and their offspring.

5 Bad Public Relations

If anyone is in any doubt that wasps are perceived as general purveyors of pain and misery, just have a little look at the Bible where a jealous and vengeful Old Testament God is wreaking chaos on the enemies of the children of Israel.

> And I will send hornets before thee, which shall drive out the Hivite, the Canaanite, and the Hittite, from before thee. (Exodus 23:28)

> Moreover, the lord thy god will send the hornet among them, until they that are left, and hide themselves from thee, be destroyed. (Deuteronomy 7:20)

> And I sent the hornet before you, which drave them out from before you, even the two kings of the Amorites: but not with thy sword, nor with thy bow. (Joshua 24:12)

Despite the German proverb that God made the bee but the Devil made the wasp, it seems that this God was more than happy to put the Devil's handiwork to his own nefarious use. To make things even more menacing, these hymenopteran acts of God were not a quick decisive smiting, but a lingering pestilential torture:

I will not drive them out from before thee in one year; lest the land become desolate, and the beast of the field multiply against thee.

By little and little I will drive them out from before thee, until thou be increased, and inherit the land. (Exodus 23:29–30)

We may never know what doubts the 47 scholarly translators of the King James Bible may have had when they were trying to understand the distinctions between various types of stinging insects mentioned in the Greek, Hebrew or Aramaic documents they had to hand in the early 1600s when they were tasked with their great literary work. We now know that during the Iron Age, as today, *Vespula* social wasps did not occur commonly in the biblical Middle East or North Africa. The paper (umbrella) wasp is frequent, but the oriental hornet, *Vespa orientalis*, was the dominant large-nest species, occurring throughout the area and into Asia Minor, the Arabian Peninsula and India. Hornets are large wasps, and their sting can be painful, but their size belies their much more docile nature. Nevertheless, they have obviously had an image problem for thousands of years.

IF WASPS ARE BAD, HORNETS MUST BE WORSE

Aristotle knew the difference between 'ordinary' wasps and hornets, and reported with scholarly measured tones about them attacking large blow flies around dung and lopping off their heads, eating sweet fruits and having a queen (or leader at least) much larger in proportion to the workers than in either wasps or bees. Even so, it is tempting to read some enmity into his text; despite his uncertainty about whether or not queen wasps stung, or the

Plate I

There is no escaping the fact that hornets are much larger than wasps, and that the queens are huge, but they are still handsome and regal creatures, ably portrayed in these hand-coloured engravings by E. W. Robinson from 1866.

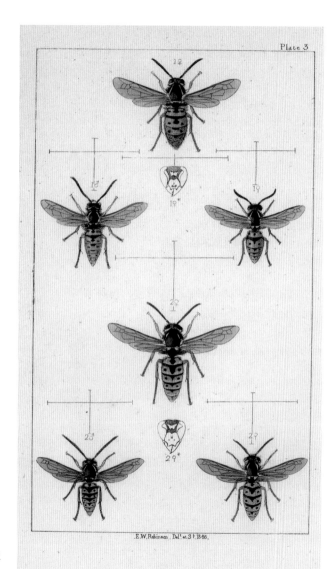

Hand-coloured engravings by E. W. Robinson, 1866.

sex of stingless worker/drones, he is confident that all hornets appear to have stings. Was he speaking from personal experience?

In 'Jubilate Agno', the poem in which Christopher Smart earlier praised the sanctified architecture of the wasp nest, he also reiterated the biblical terror of the hornet: 'Let Jehu bless with the hornet, who is the soldier of the Lord, to extirpate abomination and to prepare the way of peace.'[1] Unfortunately Smart was simply regurgitating the conventional view that hornets must be ferocious. They're not, and hornets actually make poor warriors. Unlike the smaller wasp species, *Vespula*, which can afford to go on suicidal defensive attacks and lose hundreds of workers to repel an enemy, hornets live in small colonies of only one or two hundred individuals and rely more on secreting their home in a hidden corner or high in a hollow tree branch out of reach of Winnie-the-Pooh.

The equating of size with ferocity continued well into the scientific age. When Vincenz Kollar (1797–1860) wrote what is now reckoned to be the first full modern treatise on insect pests in 1840, he introduced his chapter on those that were troublesome for their attacks on man with, 'The most dangerous of these is unquestionably the hornet – *Vespa crabro*.'[2] He offers no evidence to support this claim, just the usual discrimination that because they are the biggest wasps, then they must also be the worst. He insouciantly suggests destroying the nests with lighted brimstone.

The idea that hornets are brooding nuggets of animated animosity runs deep through folklore too. The Norfolk folk song, 'The Hornet and the Beetle', from about 1880, sets the stage with: 'The hornet set [sat] in an 'oller [old elm] tree, and a proper spiteful toad were he.'[3] It is difficult to decide who is most maligned by the comparison – the hornet or the toad? The author of the song lyrics knew nothing of wasp spite, especially given that a male hornet is, of course, stingless and incapable of harm. Meanwhile, to a generation of mid-twentieth-century film- and theatregoers, British actress Peggy Mount was one of the last of a series of time-honoured battleaxes perfectly personified in her portrayal of Emma Hornett in *Sailor Beware*, a deliberate play on words to set her up as the domineering, overwhelmingly raucous queen wasp of the otherwise quiet and sedate domestic nest.

It may have been the perceived spiteful aggressiveness that encouraged Israeli researchers to give hornets (*V. orientalis* again) LSD and amphetamines. This was the 1960s when dropping acid or speed onto unsuspecting wild animals was an acceptable pastime, but contrary to the peace, love and understanding that normally reigns in a hornet colony, the drugs elicited increased aggression, even between normally peaceable sisterly nestmates.

The misinformation continues. Jimi Hendrix's 'Hornets Nest' (1966) buzzes with urgent and angry guitar wails to give a threatening edgy sound. In reality hornets are much quieter – a contented low baritone hum. The idea of stirring up a hornets' nest has been

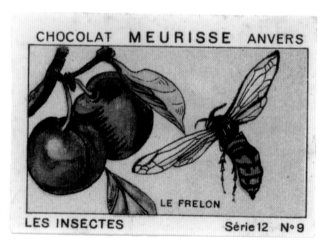

Collector's card by the French chocolate manufacturer Meurisse, showing a hornet (*frelon*) making an attack on some ripe plums. In fact wasps and hornets really only feed on damaged or windfall fruit.

RUNNING AMUCK.

Cover of *Puck* magazine from November 1904, when Russia seemed to be running amok – its ambitions over Manchuria and Korea led to the Russo–Japanese War and the following year there was a national uprising and revolution. The wasp, representing Japan, perhaps signifies Russia's misguided flailings.

around in metaphor since the end of the seventeenth century, but it still does a disservice to these elegant and gentle giants. Thomas Muffet, writing in the sixteenth century, tells in misogynistic terms of when he 'stirred up a hornet, to shew the nature of women when they are angry, the more you strive with them, the more you provoke them'.[4] The third novel by the successful Swedish writer Stieg Larsson was originally titled *Luftslottet som sprängdes* (2007), literally 'the air castle that was blown up', but acquired a catchier and more mellifluous title in English: *The Girl who Kicked the Hornets' Nest*. In truth no hornets' nest is ever within kicking reach, and most are even out of observation reach, high up in hollow trees and branches where their occupants carry on their lives carefully, honestly, patiently.

Anyone who has ever properly examined a hornets' nest at close quarters, without kicking it or stirring it, will concur that the largest of wasps has the smallest of tempers. This lovely anecdote from Edwardian naturalist and writer Edward Step illustrates this so well:

> Precipitately descending a woodland bank, whose slope was more acute than we had reckoned, we checked our speed by throwing an arm around a dead birch. But the apparent tree was merely a shell of bark: the wood had all decayed, and a community of hornets had taken possession of the shell. Our weight and speed snapped it low down. In a moment there was a small cloud of excited hornets buzzing above the wreck, instead of around our head as might have been expected, and there seemed to be a sharp note of anger in the buzz. As quickly as possible, we set the birch carcase upright on its base again, and backed away slowly and quietly. To our great surprise – and relief – we were not followed: the interest of the insects was centred in their home . . . as though they were considering ways and means of remedying the disaster . . . we were not followed by a single hornet.[5]

Step had earlier castigated anyone who regarded the hornet as a dangerous beast, suggesting, 'The risk of attack by it is mostly self-created by those who get into a panic when they see it.' These pleading reports do little to assuage the fears of the general populace though, who have ever been wary of any creature they perceive as actively pursuing them; wasps and hornets were obviously fuelled by pernicious intent. This is at odds with a general perception of larger and more dangerous animals. If chased by a lion or a rhinoceros or a bull, the feeling is that the pursued

Exquisite painting of a wasp nest by famed nature artist Edward Julius Detmold (1883–1957), who illustrated the English composite translation of French entomologist Jean-Henri Fabre's *Book of Insects* (1921).

is perhaps fair game and that the victim should have been more careful and not have provoked the obviously savage animal in the first place. For something as small as a wasp to attack a person though, well, that just showed a mean streak in the insect. In antiquity, various invertebrate behaviours were explained in terms of emotion or personality. Scorpions were the worst, seen as malignant, but mosquitoes were deliberate in their stealth. Wasps, it transpires, are quick-tempered, irritable and unpredictable. Fair enough. It was these traits that inspired Aristophanes to write his play *The Wasps*, which satirized the litigious Athenians and the cantankerous wasp-like behaviour of a semi-professional jury bustling protectively around the accused – one of their own. Vaughan Williams's incidental music for the play (1909) opens

Selection of transformation cards, illustrated by Tony Meeuwissen, where the coloured pips of the cards are incorporated into a graphic design. Among many other animals, wasps are represented on the three and four of spades.

with a few bars of buzzing violins, but otherwise there is little connection with wasps; perhaps he didn't want to alienate or agitate his audience.

From one of the several ancient Greek words for wasps (, *sphex*) spheksophobia, fear of wasps, is at least partially justified by the fact that they can sting if provoked. But like all phobias, the irrational has overcome the sensible, and since time before memory wasps have been denigrated, vilified and feared beyond their diminutive measure. Once a wasp (or a hornet) has been identified as an enemy, or a pest, or in some cases elevated to the status of being just plain evil, it can be swatted with impunity, leaving no stain on the conscience.

The association of wasps with evil has a long and ignoble history. In Geoffrey Chaucer's *Prioress's Tale* (1387–1400), he combines their unholy reputation with the widespread anti-Semitic feelings of the day to denounce: 'Our first fo, the serpent Sathanas [Satan], that hath in Jewes herte his waspes nest.' The idea of a wasp nest for a heart is the perfect metaphor for cold cruelty, malevolence or unfeeling numbness. In the folk story of the heartless giant he hides his real heart in a locked box and uses a wasp nest in its place in his body so he cannot be killed. In UK indie rock band Tellison's anti-romantic break-up song, the singer's heart is a wasps' nest – in other words, he now feels nothing. Elizabeth Barrett Browning also uses the wasp as a cold metaphor in her poem 'Discontent': 'Let a frost, or a small wasp have crept to the innermost of our ripe peach.' The cold ruthlessness of the individual wasp is also used to effect, but someone should take Alex T. Smith to task for casting wasps (which in truth are actually stylish and attractive) as the ugly stepsisters in his insect retelling of the Cinderella story – *Ella the Ladybird*.[6] Of course, it was also inevitable that wasps would feature in Monty Python's alternative hymn, 'All Things Dull and Ugly':

> Each little snake that poisons,
> Each little wasp that stings,
> He made their brutish venom,
> He made their horrid wings.

If not evil personified, wasps are frequently represented as worthless, lacking any praiseworthy traits – unlike those smug honeybees who are everywhere lauded as industrious, creative and wholesome. It was a commonly repeated assumption, first detailed by Plutarch, Lucian and Tertullian, that wasps were

Gulliver had to combat wasps as big as eagles when he visited Brobdingnag. This illustration from a 1909 edition of Jonathan Swift's novel was painted by Arthur Rackham.

somehow degenerate bees, as if their miserable lives were a self-inflicted consequence of having failed to keep up with the morally virtuous hive work ethic. Charles Dickens uses them to paint a picture of indolence and decay in the French Flemish country where his *Uncommercial Traveller*, trying to stock up on face-wash toiletries, found the shops empty and counters bare: 'the wasps, who seemed to have taken military possession of the town, and to have placed it under wasp-martial law, executed warlike manoeuvres in the windows. Other shops the wasps had entirely to themselves, and nobody cared.'[7] Nobody cared to answer him tapping his five-franc coin on the counter either, and in the end he had to pass the evening spongeless.

It is, of course, late summer when wasps start to make themselves more obvious. This is the time that they visit the picnic table or the cream tea, or the French Flemish shop windows. With no brood to care for in the nest, and no nutritious droplets of larval regurgitation to sate their sweet tooth, the workers wander aimlessly, finding nourishment in the human cakes and jams thoughtfully laid out for them.

One wasp flying around the sandwiches is enough to send some people scuttling for shelter. In the national parks of Washington state, the nuisance level is quantifiable, with seven to ten wasps per hour being the rate at which park rangers start to receive complaints from visitors.[8] It is hard to imagine what picnickers think the rangers will do though, other than stick up a few wasp traps to catch and drown the offending insects. Such traps have been used since time immemorial, especially around beehives or in orchards and vineyards. Aelian suggested a cage with a small fish inside it to attract the wasps, but a jar half-filled with beer, cider or watered-down jam is now standard.[9] Charles Lamb (1775–1834) immortalized such traps in his poem 'Wasps in a Garden':

He peeps in the narrow-mouthed glass,
Which depends from the branch of a tree;
He ventures to creep down, – alas!
To be drowned in that delicate sea.[10]

This response would be met with horror for almost any other animal, but it is OK to mindlessly kill wasps, especially when we can't be bothered, yet again, to realize that they are all female. Most of the killing is pointless anyway because the majority of picnics actually go off quite happily without wasps interfering. Evidence for this is clear from a recent feature in *The Guardian* on the top ten picnics in art;[11] no matter how closely the works by Manet (*Le Déjeuner sur l'herbe*), Titian (*The Pastoral Concert*), Rubens (*Peace and War*) and others are examined, not one wasp can be found. Not one.

If they do come, though, just squish 'em. George Orwell was more than happy to publish his tale of wasp torturing, knowing that nobody would write to the editor and complain of his brutality:

I thought of a rather cruel trick I once played on a wasp. He was sucking jam on my plate, and I cut him in half. He paid no attention, merely went on with his meal, while a tiny stream of jam trickled out of his severed oesophagus. Only when he tried to fly away did he grasp the dreadful thing that had happened to him.[12]

Some pedantic entomologist should have written to complain that Orwell had sexed his wasp victim incorrectly.

Wasp torture and execution play a central role in Iain Banks's first novel *The Wasp Factory*.[13] The 'factory' is a mechanism put together by the novel's psychopathic protagonist Frank Cauldhame;

behind the twelve numerals on a large clock face twelve different deaths await the victim wasp introduced through a central hole. Cauldhame somehow believes that the death 'chosen' by the wasp, by crushing, burning, drowning in urine or whatever, is a portent of future events. The novel was greeted with a mixture of acclaim and disgust at the graphic descriptions of gruesome violence – mostly to mice, dogs and small children, rather than to the poor wasps.

At the more tawdry end of the film special-effects spectrum, wasps don't even have to look like wasps to be labelled as the enemy. In the ghastly sci-fi horror B-movie *Monster from Green Hell* (1957), an experimental space rocket carrying wasps malfunctions, flies off course and crashes in Africa after the occupants are exposed to cosmic radiation. The resulting green metallic monsters, the size of houses, are about as wasp-like as winged dinosaurs, but constant scripted mentions of 'insect', 'stinger', 'nest' and 'queen' try to keep the plot on track. Almost sixty years later, in what was billed as a horror comedy (*Stung*, 2015), it is toxic plant fertilizer that encourages subterranean wasps, likely to be all-black spider-killing wasps, to grow 2 metres long and cause mayhem at a posh, country-house garden party. Even to the expert entomologist the antagonist insects don't look very vespine, but short, sharp editing and constant cries of 'WASP!' helpfully inform the audience what the creatures that appear on screen are meant to be. In the end, of course, all the wasps, green or black, meet their natural or unnatural ends. Wasp death is inevitable and grief free.

According to at least one published psychological study, to dream about killing a wasp signifies the dreamer's fearless ability to stand up to enemies – though the authors sceptically admit they are quoting a rather flaky new-age source.[14] Again, the wasp is straightforwardly presented as the baddie and its destruction the inevitable just act of a righteous mind.

The wasp baddie, as portrayed on a postcard from the First World War. Produced by Géligné in Paris, this is one of a series where the Allies are depicted as beautiful girls/butterflies, with wings in the patterns of national flags. The four Central Powers nations are Austria, shown here as a Franz Joseph wasp; Bulgaria as a bumblebee; Turkey as a cockchafer and Germany as a stag beetle, all pinned through with swords and all with the heads of their male national leaders.

Autriche

Justifiable persecution of wasps is set to continue if neo-noir science-fiction film *Blade Runner* (1982) is to be believed. In a dystopian future world (ironically set now, in 2019) where the only way to distinguish between real humans and genetically engineered replicant androids is to elicit emotional responses, the hero of the movie, Decker (played by Harrison Ford) quizzes the seemingly fragile and painfully beautiful Rachael (Sean Young). Asked what she would do if a child showed her his butterfly collection, Rachael answers deadpan that she would take him to see a doctor. What if a wasp landed on her? Without hesitation, she'd kill it. So that's all right then. Mind you, it turns out that she's a replicant after all, maybe casting doubt on the validity of her philosophical judgements on the life or death of an insect.

Mostly, wherever wasps are portrayed, they are picked out as the baddies. However, it's pleasing to note that Richard Rodgers and Oscar Hammerstein II tried to redress the issue slightly in *The Sound of Music* by having Julie Andrews sing about dogs biting and bees, rather than wasps, stinging. Bees do sting, and they can be a right nuisance. Worse than wasps even.

Today, any Internet search for 'wasps' brings up, top of the list, a slew of pest-control companies itching to get their chemical sprays and flame-throwers on the colony that is obviously causing problems simply by deigning to exist. Many of these show videos of the pest controller in action with manly all-in-one protective overalls, hat-and-veil face coverings, and vespine carnage all around. The message is loud and clear – killing wasps is not only fine, it is expected of any upright law-abiding citizen. Why else would the *Wasp!* swatting game app have been developed for those idle moments spent on a smart phone? 'Swat all the wasps by touching them within the time before you get stung.' Worse:

Rather forbiddingly entitled 'Slaughter of the innocents', this plate from Edward Step's *Marvels of Insect Life* (1915) purports to show mass wasp infanticide. Wasps are known to take their own grubs at the end of the season, but this is probably opportunistic cannibalism rather than orchestrated butchery.

Save the Bee – Kill the Wasp is also available from the app store. This is, however, at least legal. Sir George Sitwell (1860–1943, father of poet Edith) was reputed to own a miniature pistol to shoot at passing wasps. More than sixty years after his death, this anecdote was brought up again when *The Telegraph* published a 'readers' guide to the fine art of killing a wasp', which included shooting at them with airgun pellets, hosing them down with water, snipping them in half with embroidery scissors, and poisoning them with neat gin. The piece was accompanied by a faux-Edwardian *Punch*-style cartoon just to show what jolly fun it all was.

Wasps, it seems, have few friends willing to protest their mass murder. Having said this, there was something of an outcry when citizen science project the Big Wasp Survey was launched in 2017 and promoted on BBC's *Countryfile*. The idea was to trap (and kill) wasps in a homemade beer trap, made of a cut-up plastic drinks bottle, and send the specimens off to the laboratory so that species make-up, population numbers and geographic spread could be monitored year on year. The idea of seemingly thoughtless slaughter riled some commentators, though similar wasp traps are common above patios throughout the country and widely used by bee-keepers to keep the useless wasps away from their hardworking hero bees. Some self-editing of publicity and press releases followed and the project has, after all, gone ahead well; results are now awaited with interest. The anticipated takeup will have resulted in a few thousand wasps from all over the country being sacrificed to the very worthwhile and carefully thought-through scientific study, while calling out the pest controller to just a single loft nest would have dispatched a similar number in an afternoon, purely for the selfish sake of one anxious householder. There was more than a little over dramatic tabloid trouble-stirring, many of which publications no doubt went on to bemoan terrible wasp plagues a few months later.

If there could possibly be any doubt that the world hates wasps, then it is now official – proved scientifically. Just as this book was going to press a paper in the esteemed scientific journal *Ecological Entomology* explained 'Why We Love Bees and Hate Wasps'.[15] The universal dislike of wasps was absolutely clear from the results of a questionnaire answered by nearly 750 members of the public, who mainly associated wasps with negative words like 'sting', 'angry' and 'annoying', while bees engendered positive notions of 'honey', 'pollination', 'buzz' and 'flowers'. The multi-billion-dollar international honeybee lobby has successfully indoctrinated the world, and the perceived value of bees in pollination services, honey production and generally being upright and industrious is firmly cemented. Meanwhile the worth of wasps as apex predators, useful pollinators and an intrinsic part of a rich biodiversity is completely lost. There are, perhaps, no surprises here, but the authors do not simply blame an ill-informed public: they suggest that insect scientists could do much more of the informing – supporting wasps and improving the insects' undeserved reputations. Scientific research, it turns out, is also wildly skewed towards studies on honeybees, creating a self-enhancing cycle of increasing bee research as funding follows publication output, which in turn follows funding sources. Wasp research, however, remains in the doldrums, a peripheral diminishing sub-topic attracting limited support from disinterested funding bodies. By promoting research into their behaviours and life cycles, entomologists should be enthusing about wasps, explaining their biological significance in the landscape and reiterating just why wasps are so fascinating and important. Well, we live in hope.

6 Tabloid Mayhem

Why is it that wasps get such bad press? Blame the media. Every spring, newspaper editors watch their gardens come alive with bumblebees, honeybees and butterflies frolicking in the shy slanting sunlight and everything is well with the world. They don't notice the few lone queen wasps carefully and assiduously constructing their embryo nests in deep corners and foraging for early hoverflies and bluebottles. But come late July, and with a taste for cream teas, these same editors now start to see the wasps. Suddenly these insects are everywhere and something has to be done about it. Inevitably someone is stung, a huge paper nest is found in a spare bedroom. Cue the usual spate of nonsense wasp plague headlines.

In this thoroughly urban age, people have become estranged from the natural environment. In Britain, this surge into cities came with the industrial revolution, so the disjunct with nature has been going on for 250 years. This is why an urban populace now understands so little about wildlife, and gives far too much credence to the tabloids. So it is that each year jarring headlines are spawned to whip up a lather over giant Euro-wasps and invading killer hornets from the Far East. All it takes is one bad reaction to a sting to set the outrage ball rolling.

Polistes (probably *metricus*) nest under the eaves of a Florida house. Unfortunately the Internet is filled with stories of foolish people destroying these small exposed nests by hurling rocks or baseballs at them, then wondering why the wasps sting.

IT ONLY TAKES ONE STING

Despite the almost infinitesimal dose of sting venom, there is always a danger that the body's response will be more than a mild swelling. A very small minority of people react to a wasp (or bee!) sting, not by a local reaction in the skin immediately around the wound, but systemically. Their whole body convulses from the catastrophic cascade of immunological reactions that lead to anaphylactic shock. Every death from a wasp sting is a terrible tragedy, but it is beneath contempt that it should be used by the media to fuel an ignorant and useless war on these insects.

Anaphylaxis is a sudden, huge and overwhelming immuno-logical reaction. Like most allergies it usually starts with the body being sensitized to some alien chemical. By analogy, this is the body's normal reaction to diseases, and is why humans normally only get measles, say, or chickenpox, the once. The first attack is dealt with and at the same time the body is sensitized to the invading organisms. If another invasion threatens months or years later the body is ready with tailored antigens to knock it back in a sudden and violent defence. This is also why vaccination

Anaphylaxis is the body's overwhelming physiological response to just a single sting, but multiple stings are also dangerous. This, though, is a fictional, stereotyped image.

works, by pre-priming that antigen defence. Human bodies can sometimes get it wrong, however, and spurious substances like insect venom, foods or pharmaceuticals can lead to the sudden body-wide release of histamines and other inflammatory proteins. These lead to constriction of muscles in the lungs causing breathing difficulties, vasodilation leading to sudden low blood pressure, interference with heart muscles and internal bleeding. Reactions can be rapid, causing collapse within ten to fifteen minutes and unless treated with emergency medical care (usually adrenaline injection) death can swiftly follow. In known reports of fatalities from wasp venom anaphylaxis, 66 per cent of victims were dead within one hour and 95 per cent were dead within five hours. Each sudden devastating death from a wasp sting, seemingly out of proportion to the animal's size, only furthers the ill feeling towards wasps. Thankfully, such deaths are very rare indeed. In one of the first in-depth scientific studies of deaths from Hymenoptera stings only 12 per cent were actually from anaphylaxis; 70 per cent were from stings in the throat causing airway blockage.[1]

The earliest supposed recorded death from wasp-sting anaphylaxis was in 2641 BC when, according to the hieroglyphs surmounting his tomb, King Menes died mysteriously after a hornet sting. This tale is parroted through history, allergy and wasp textbooks alike, but is likely to be a complete myth. It appears that the ancient Egyptian hieroglyph word for hippopotamus has the same value as that for wasp, and the ebony plates on which the markings were found are very poorly preserved.[2] Death by hippopotamus is much more likely, and still a real danger in parts of Africa, although they no longer occur in the River Nile or the Nile delta.

Early reports of anaphylaxis did not understand the science behind the deaths, but these rare tragedies punctuate the textbooks, adding a worrying random uncertainty to the already painful attack. Vincenz Kollar, writing his first pest control handbook in 1840, quotes examples of men dying, and others suffering: 'inflammatory fever, fainting, fits and convulsions' although these were from honeybee stings more often than wasp.[3]

A seemingly huge nest in a London loft space. Although the size of a beach ball, this was really quite modest, with just seven combs and about 3,000 brood cells. It was long disused, and the bird nesting material between the rafters from generations of starlings was much more of a problem.

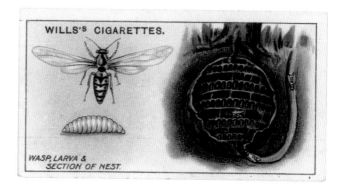

Number 41 in a series of fifty cigarette cards depicting garden life, 1914, mainly telling us how bad wasps are at attacking and spoiling 'all varieties of fruit' and how best to destroy the nests using sulphur or gunpowder.

The science behind anaphylaxis was teased out in the early twentieth century, after Charles Richet and Paul Portier tried to isolate Portuguese man-of-war venom and develop a prophylactic treatment against the painful stings. After priming, they noticed that a tiny amount could subsequently elicit breathing difficulties and death in their test dogs. Richet was awarded a Nobel Prize for Medicine in 1913. Those sudden deaths from wasp stings could now be explained scientifically. It wasn't long before the science started to make appearances in non-scientific literature. In her 1935 novel *Death in the Clouds*, Agatha Christie's first red herring was a red mark on the corpse and a wasp flying around the cabin of the aeroplane. Luckily Belgian detective Hercule Poirot soon dismisses anaphylaxis as a possible cause of death (spoiler alert: the victim was poisoned). Nevertheless, the wasp made an interesting distraction, and duly featured in hugely out-of-proportion size against the small propeller plane on the cover of several paperback editions. Later the same wasp appeared in true giant size as a shape-shifting alien life form in the *Doctor Who* episode 'The Unicorn and the Wasp' (2008). Set in 1926 during the mysterious but well-known eleven-day disappearance of Christie, it suggested the later-erased memory of the giant alien wasp resurfaced as a trope in her book many years afterwards. Sadly, the more prosaic explanation of Christie's inspiration following Richet's discovery is not explored by the Time Lord.

Anaphylaxis can result from many different allergic responses. Based on an analysis of 214 fatalities in 1992–2001, each year in the UK there are about four deaths following bee and wasp stings.[4] But this is compared to about six deaths a year from food allergies (famously peanuts) and nine from pharmaceuticals. Deaths from the animated, and therefore obviously intentful wasps are projected as evil, malicious, devious and spiteful, whereas those from food or drug responses are seen merely as unfortunate accidents. Wait till the foreign wasps get here, though.

FOREIGN INVADERS

In August 1980 entomologist Steven Falk found an unusual-looking wasp in Friston Forest near Eastbourne. It was a lone male, but was as large as the queens of other British species and turned out to be *Dolichovespula media*, a species not hitherto recorded on these islands.[5] It was originally named *media* by virtue of being intermediate in size between the common wasp, *Vespula vulgaris* and the hornet, *Vespa crabro*; indeed, the huge queens, which are marked with orange and brown as well as black and yellow look remarkably hornet-like. Before long, colonies were found along the south coast and it started to spread. Today it is found widely across England and lowland Wales, and is making inroads into Scotland.

If ordinary wasps have a bad reputation, the median wasp, as it is now called, has four extra black marks against its name: it is much larger than our native wasps, making it more obvious; the workers are often very dark, sometimes with bodies nearly entirely black, making them more obvious; it makes aerial nests hanging in hedgerows making them more obvious; and it is obviously foreign. When *media* arrived the media had a field day. Regular headlines warned of Euro-invaders, super-wasps, new killer wasps, swarmageddon, waspzilla. It was clear that the most sensationalist articles were written by people who knew nothing about wasps. All the usual ecological errors were spouted again; many commentators couldn't even work out what species they were talking about. It didn't help that Britain's two commonest species are *Vespula vulgaris*, the 'common' wasp, and *Vespula germanica*, the 'German' wasp. But it is only German on the basis that the species was originally described as different from *vulgaris*, by a Dane (Johan Christian Fabricius) in 1793, based on specimens he had received from a correspondent in Poland, which is near Germany. In fact *Vespula vulgaris* and *Vespula germanica* are equally common and more or less ubiquitous across most of Britain and much of Ireland, indeed well into Eurasia.

Of course the foreign invader super-wasps, whether median or German, were always disparaged in the tabloids for having more painful stings, being generally more aggressive, usually out of work (at the end of the year when there was no brood-rearing to get on with) and often being 'drunk' on fallen fruit, like some ghastly band of unruly Continental football supporters. It's a wonder the median wasp survived in Britain, given all the hostility it received.

Something odd seems to have been happening in the European wasp world during the 1980s, because in 1987 another 'new' wasp, *Dolichovespula saxonica* was also found in the UK for the first time, in Dorking, Surrey.[6] During the 1990s the first nests were found in East Anglia, and this species too has spread across much of Britain, building its delicately compact aerial nests in trees and bushes in parks and gardens across the land. This one dropped well below the media radar though; it was hardly newsworthy to point out that a Saxon wasp now occurred in the land of the Anglo-Saxons.

Luckily for story-starved news editors, a new threat is now available, thanks to the imminent arrival of the Asian hornet *Vespa velutina*. Though smaller than the native European hornet, *velutina* has made a nuisance of itself in France after it was accidentally introduced from the Far East in 2004. Hibernating females had arrived in terracotta pots from China and it quickly became obvious that the species had established well beyond any possible eradication measures. It soon spread to Spain (2010), Belgium (2011), Portugal (2011), Italy (2013) and the Channel Islands (2016). This time the danger was not to humans, but to honeybees, the favoured prey of this Far Eastern wasp.

Now take your tabloid statistics in any order you like. A single hornet can dispatch 25 to thirty honeybees a day, and an unfeasible forty in a minute according to one provocative news website. A hornet colony can destroy an entire beehive in four hours, or perhaps it is two hours. First they kill all the adult bees and then they remove the brood to feed to their own grubs. Honeybees could be wiped out within twenty years. Food shortages will follow. It's the end of civilization as we know it. All those dreadful anti-wasp headlines reappeared, but this time bigger. Even *The Times* described it as another 'super-wasp'.

All this was a bit academic since the hornet had not yet crossed into the UK. That didn't stop news organizations wringing their hands and proclaiming that the end was nigh. When no Asian hornets obligingly turned up, reports concentrated on explaining the possibility that they might arrive here at any moment and repeating the dire warnings, while busily illustrating their pieces with photos of ordinary hornets that people thought might have been Asian, but actually weren't. At least the native hornet got a bit of positive publicity; by comparison it was seen as fascinating and awe-inspiring, if still huge and a bit scary.

All this changed in September 2016, though, when a genuine Asian hornet was seen foraging around an apiary in Tetbury, Gloucestershire, and a nest was found nearby. Luckily it was quickly destroyed and a search of the area produced no more colonies, but another specimen was collected the following year in north Somerset, and at the time of writing, February 2019, there have been thirteen confirmed sightings and six nests have been destroyed. Britain's bee-keepers, entomologists and journalists now wait on tenterhooks. The public have been warned to look out for the insects and helpful information sheets are available to download from pest-control and bee-keeping websites. As this book goes to press the jury is still out as to whether the Asian hornet will become permanently established in Britain. If it does, will anything change?

ALL WASPS EAT BEES ANYWAY

Despite the reputation that precedes them, Asian hornets are not the only honeybee-eating wasps. Honeybees make tasty protein-rich meals for many predatory insects, with the added bonus of a stomach full of sweet energy-giving nectar too. Both *Vespula vulgaris* and *Vespula germanica* have long been known for their exploitation of honeybees given half a chance. Anthony Fitzherbert, writing his sixteenth-century agricultural treatise *Boke of Husbandrie* warned, 'And beware that noo waspes come into the hyve, for they wyll kyl the bees and eate the honny.'[7] In a rare outburst of ecological knowledge, Shakespeare (*Two Gentlemen of Verona*, 1.2) knew of 'injurious wasps, to feed on such sweet honey, and kill the bees that yield it'. In *The Rape of Lucrece* he later imbued the honey-feeding wasp with moral theft: 'In thy weak hive a wandering wasp hath crept, and suck'd the honey which thy chaste bee kept.' Additionally Alfred Tennyson complained of 'wasps in our good hive'.[8]

When these wasps (*Vespula germanica* in particular) were first discovered introduced into North America and New Zealand it was their depredations on hives rather than their stinging of humans that got them their first bit of bad press.[9] In Britain, though, honeybees and wasps wage a constant but measured war against each other. An aquatint by Graham Sutherland, *Expulsion and Killing of an Enemy* (1976), shows a wasp being expelled and killed by three honeybees, in laudably correct anatomic detail all round. It came to the fore in 2006 when it was one of the nation's works of art chosen by Gordon Brown to decorate the walls of the treasury when he was chancellor of the exchequer. The press speculated that his enemy was Tony Blair, who had thus far failed to honour his pledge to step down as prime minister to make way for Mr Brown.[10] Nearby, Mr Brown hung a print by George Francis Joseph of Spencer Perceval, the only British prime minister ever to have been assassinated. It was all very pointed.

In the Near East, the biblical hornet *Vespa orientalis* has also long been known as a nuisance around beehives – perhaps that was how God swept away the enemies of the Israelites, by sending hornets to ruin their honeybee stocks and decimate their pollination services industry. In Japan the giant hornet, *Vespa mandarinia*, one of the world's biggest species, is a veritable scourge, but bee-keepers there get along just fine.

Not every wasp loitering near a hive is up to no good – they are superlative scavengers too. Naturalist and pioneer wildlife photographer Richard Kearton reports:

Wasps are exceedingly interesting creatures to study. They visit my beehive in search of any unconsidered trifle they can pick up, and it does not appear to matter whether they find the newly thrown out body of a drone or a member of their own species, it is cut up and carried away to their nests for the benefit of their voracious larvae.[11]

At least there is genuine evidence that Asian hornets are a real problem for European bee-keepers, and it is not all fear-mongering blather after all. *Vespa velutina* is a specialist at dispatching bees, having evolved in India, Southeast Asia and China to attack the eastern honeybee *Apis cerana*. This is slightly smaller than the western honeybee *Apis mellifera*, the domesticated species that now produces the vast bulk of honey for human consumption through Europe, North Africa, the Americas and Australasia. Having evolved without reference to a formidable predator, *mellifera* is unused to defending itself against this new enemy. The honeybee's sting, so potent against humans or grizzly bears, does not seem able to penetrate the hornet's carapace. The devastating hive attacks happen with complete impunity. In the Far East, though, the eastern honeybees have evolved a completely different tactic to repel the hornets. A ball of *Apis cerana* workers, fifty to a hundred of them, envelop the attacking wasp and overpower it by the joint metabolic heat generated from their individually diminutive bodies, now combined into one fighting ball of hot anger, effectively frying it alive. Many bees die too, but the colony can afford the cannon fodder losses to control the hornet attacks to an acceptable and sustainable level. *Apis mellifera* has yet to adopt this strategy.

In the meantime, any Asian hornet nests found in the British Isles must be sought out and destroyed. Perhaps a technique gleaned from the letters pages of *The Times* during the 1970s might be useful in locating their nests. The first correspondent wrote of their tried and tested method:

caught a wasp on the window pane, covered it with flour and released it out of doors . . . it would immediately return to its nest. This it did, zooming in a straight line to the local river bank, with myself and a friend running underneath the flour-coated insect. Today 40 years later, I tried the same method. The wasp flew some 30 yards and disappeared into its nest. Possibly some of your country readers, plagued by wasps, may care to try this. It's a certainty!

It wasn't long, though, before potential holes were reported in this sure-fire procedure:

I caught one just now, devouring an expensive peach. I covered it, and myself, with large quantities of flour. I descended from a great height to street level and released the insect. It did not return directly to its nest. It rose vertically and vanished towards the sun. I returned to my flat. That same white wasp was once again lunching on that same peach. How can one destroy a creature with a sense of humour?

And later, mockery:

I caught my wasp and coated it with flour. Then I ran down the garden beneath the whitened creature. Unfortunately it soared over a ten-foot wall. I was not so agile. When my bruises are healed I shall try again, but this time using self-raising flour, on myself as well as the wasp.[12]

All very amusing, and the usual British sarcasm is probably well warranted. Oriental hornets are recorded as flying at 2.6–3.8

metres (8.5–12.5 ft) per second (9.3–13.7 km, or 5.8–8.5 mi., per hour),[13] and although this is about half the speed measured for honeybees making their celebrated bee-lines, it's still questionable how far a pursuer might be able to follow and still keep one in sight. Others have tried tying a short piece of cotton thread to a wasp, to slow it down and make it more visible as it flies. This has inherent flaws in that the wasp frequently becomes tangled, or refuses to get airborne as it tries to groom itself free of its encumbrance.

The usual technique employed by hymenopterists to locate wasp nests is to leave out some sweet food bait and then try to visually determine where the constant airborne trail of wasps coming and going actually comes from and goes to. This is the equivalent of following the busy motorway rather than trying to keep tabs on any individual car.

IT WASN'T ALWAYS THIS WAY

In the modern world, death is polarized. For almost all living things, death is viewed with sadness or regret – unless we're talking about wasps, in which case they deserve it. But this is a recent sentiment. Read any popular book up to about the mid-twentieth century and wasps are reported in measured prose. Yes, many times specimens are killed and their nests are destroyed, but big game hunting, butterfly collecting and whaling all too ended with death as the ethically acceptable outcome of the times. These were all reported in the same matter-of-fact tone because they were all part of the same ethos of nature – that it was perfectly acceptable for humans to subdue, exploit or kill the creatures out there, be it for commercial gain, scientific advancement, appreciation of the omniscient creator or private erudition through nature study.

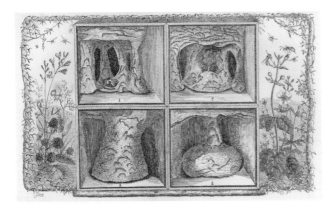

Though paying lip-service to the wonderment of wasp architecture, there is also an air of threat in the alien constructions unearthed and depicted in Rev. J. G. Wood's *Homes without Hands* (1866).

Wasps were part of that natural world, which was fascinating to look at and learn from. How many newspaper reports or web articles would now describe wasps as 'splendidly painted with bars of gold and black'?[14] They were really no more persecuted than other animals, and if a colony had to be destroyed it was with a certain degree of regret. John Henry Comstock wrote a textbook of entomology which remained the standard work for u.s. undergraduates for nearly fifty years; in it he reluctantly recalls: 'On one occasion I found a fine large nest under the base-board of one of my bee-hives, and into which I inadvertently thrust my toes, with sad results, while examining the hive. The nest is now in the Cornell [University Museum] collection.'[15]

Edward Step, in his *Insect Artizans and their Work* (1919), devotes a whole chapter to paper-makers (social wasps) and lovingly describes how the queen wasp tends to the larvae in her embryo nest, 'capturing flies and other insects, masticating the soft parts and feeding the grubs from mouth to mouth, much as a bird feeds her callow nestlings'.[16] Throughout the popular literature there are frequent references to 'the little architects' who are 'industrious' and 'devote themselves with ardour to the task', whilst

Hydrotherapy (or the 'water cure'), a therapy in which water was believed to penetrate cracks in the skin and flush out impurities and toxins. Along with sea bathing, it enjoyed a revival in the mid-19th century but was frequently mocked for being dubious quack medicine, as in this engraving from 1869.

Pry'd & Pub by Newman & Co

May 1869.

48 Watling St London.

JUST AS THE DOCTOR HAS FIXED ME IN MY ARM AND LEG
BATH. A WASP THREATENS TO SETTLE ON MY NOSE.

Nº 12.

'tender although irritable nurses lavish their attention in a most affectionate manner'.[17] Admittedly these publications are at the more cerebral end of the popular readership spectrum, but a similar tone can be found in the sometimes cloying prose of the 'juvenile', the burgeoning genre of illustrated Victorian books produced by a rapidly mechanizing print industry for a knowledge-thirsty populace. This is exactly the market that modern tabloid newspapers are now aimed at.

Not surprisingly, in his slightly sanctimonious celebration of animal constructions, *Homes Without Hands*, the Reverend J. G. Wood goes on at length about the 'marvel of ingenious industry' that is the wasp nest. He describes in charming terms how the queen wasp seeks out a new nest site like 'a careful matron selecting a new home', and regales us with tales of wasps snatching flies from the bellies of the totally indifferent pigs wallowing in their sty.[18] In another of his sermonizing books he further praises their architectural prowess by showing how wasps pre-empted the invention of the pillar to structure their buildings with supported floors,[19] though he perhaps says something of the age with his choice of comparative human floor-and-pillar construction which is a cross section of a slave ship showing the clever arrangement of claustrophobic cells supported on cells in which the unfortunate captives were transported.

Popular Victorian writer Arabella Buckley (author of *The Fairy-Land of Science*, so you can tell what her take will be) reiterates her wonder at 'their beautifully constructed paper nests', but concentrates on 'their helpless infants each in its cell tended with the utmost care; and we should learn almost to have an affection for these industrious creatures, which in some ways show even greater intelligence than the bees'.[20]

By the middle of the twentieth century, Arthur Mee's instructive but still rather moralizing *Children's Encyclopedia* admonishes fears of wasps: 'In practice there is little to choose between the sting of bee and wasp . . . both are highly painful and alarming to timid and susceptible people.'[21] He is pleased to invoke the Bible and clergy when he mentions wasps in his article on paper-making:

When Solomon advised the sluggard to go to the ant, he might have advised the paper-maker to go to the wasp, but no-one thought of going to the wasp till 1765, when a priest of Ratisbon, named Schäffer, began to experiment with wasps' nests and sawdust and wood shavings.[22]

True enough, Jacob Christian Schäffer is sometimes credited with being the first person to make useable paper from wood pulp, having been directly inspired by social wasps. His major monograph on paper manufacture came complete with various paper samples, including one made from reconstituted wasp nests.[23]

In an era before tabloids, a cutesy illustration from Edwin Landseer would have been enough to show how the poor old pet monkeys were in frightful danger of being stung by a horrid wasp.

Although pest-control handbooks of the time were happy to advise on the removal of nuisance nests under the eaves, many of these books did not mention wasps at all. This was a time when agricultural pests and insect disease vectors were to the fore, so titles like *The Insect Menace*, *Insect Legion* and *Insect Enemies* concentrated their ire on mosquitoes, locusts, lice, fleas, ticks and biscuit beetles rather than stinging insects. In one of the most important twentieth-century monographs on medical entomology, John Smart, keeper of entomology at London's Natural History Museum, dismissed the entire Hymenoptera in less than half a page, where he vaguely admitted that, yes, wasps can sting a bit.[24]

By comparison, today's tabloid propaganda is facile and fallacious, and boils down to a vulgar exclamation of 'Argh, burn it with fire.' Facts are garbled or invented to suit the message; statistics are twisted, experts misquoted and threats blown out of all proportion to suit the sensationalist clickbait twaddle. It doesn't help that the rest of the world is happy to go along with the easy stereotype of the grouchy stinging wasp. The visual equivalent of the stereotype tabloid wasp is the cartoon.

CARTOON WASPS ARE NO LAUGHING MATTER

A quick Google search for wasp cartoons brings up a swathe of black-and-yellow insects with thrusting pointy tails, and usually with clenched fists and a smile that is impertinent or threateningly vindictive. On the other hand, a similar search for cartoon

Engraving by Jacques Callot, c. 1622, showing Pulcinella, one of the traditional clowns of the *commedia dell'arte*, fending off a wasp attack to the usual comedic effect.

bees brings up cute, chubby, usually fluffy, doe-eyed insects waving and smiling and often carrying a bucket full of a viscous golden liquid meant to be honey. But this is how stereotypes work.

Coventry-based rugby club Wasps took their name from their striped kit, and the slightly threatening nature of the stinging insects no doubt added to their aura of power and menace on the field. Ironically, their current logo is one of the least menacing depictions of a wasp, but it still shows a highly stylized gold and black-barred insect with an uncertain number of legs and a rather diminutive eye spot. Watford Football Club and the Hornets American football team from Saline, Michigan, have similar strip colours and a history of equally dubious logos.

It doesn't help that neither anthropomorphism nor alternative colour schemes can do anything to endear wasps to us. It starts early. Take *Fifi and the Flowertots*, a UK children's stop-motion animated television series (2005–10) which follows the triumphs and tribulations of a family of flower-based fairy-type characters and a series of other garden-dwelling creatures. Bumble (AKA Fuzzbuzz) is, of course, a bumblebee, and although portrayed as clumsy is at least cheerful and helpful. Stingo the wasp, on the other hand, is grumpy and complaining. He (yes, enough said) steals food and is constantly causing trouble in the garden. If anything his cousin, the unimaginatively named Hornetto, is even nastier, and also plays a guitar. In one episode, however, the flowertots feel some sympathy for Stingo – 'wasps are a little misunderstood' – so they dress up in matching blue and yellow outfits and put on *Wasps – The Show* for him, complete with song-and-buzz routines. At least in this case Stingo was not put to painful death.

This essence of waspness personified in cartoons, logos and stylistic designs, no matter how anatomically flawed, shows just how good human brains are at abstracting the right (or wrong) information from limited data, and constructing fact or myth around what is essentially a coded message sent from the knowing designer to the recognizing mind. It's a bit like seeing a humanoid face in the windows and door of a house front or imagining the shape of the Madonna and Child in a piece of slightly burnt toast. With a few lines and a splash of the right colours, the idea 'wasp' can be promulgated and exploited – the wasp brand is born.

7   What is the Point of Wasps?

Dylan Thomas wondered deeply about the worth of wasps. Although we are not told which authors wrote them, among the 'useful' presents he received were 'books that told me everything about the wasp, except why'.[1] Every entomologist will have tales of being cornered by a member of the non-cognoscenti public, friend or stranger, asking, 'What is, actually, the point of wasps?' To the biologist this is a nonsense. The 'point' of any living organism is to eat (and not be eaten), grow and reproduce – to make more of itself by producing offspring. If it fails to do this the species would soon become extinct. Wasps are very good at making more wasps, despite the 99.9 per cent failure rate of overwintering queens. But to the layperson this question really means, 'How do wasps fit into the ecological web and balance of the world?' What they do, though, is lace their enquiry with that very human question about purpose and the point of existence, and particularly the biblical notion that all things in creation, no matter how small or noisome, were created by an omniscient creator and that he or she must have had some reason.

More often than not the question also raises the spectre of the idea that the natural world is there for humankind to use and exploit. The 'point' of a rabbit is to be a pet, or to end up in the stew; the point of four rabbits is to make a felt hat.[2] Becoming more abstruse, the point of butterflies might be to titillate the eye and uplift the soul, the point of spiders might be to catch and control flies which would otherwise spread dirt and disease, the point of bees is to pollinate flowers and give us honey. But wasps? Again, too much emphasis is put on the sting and the idea that the sting's sole purpose is to give pain to people. A dyed-in-the-wool creationist might argue that biting and stinging creatures were God's ongoing punishment for the original sin of Adam and Eve – this merely re-emphasizes the battle between humans (good, or at least misunderstood) and wasps (evil, heartless, spawn of the devil).

In earlier times wasps were considered portents of doom – a useful but not particularly attractive trait. According to Roman historian Livy (Titus Livius Patavinus, *c.* 60 BC–AD 15), a wasp swarm settled in the Temple of Mars in the southern city of Capua in 190 BC. They were gathered up and solemnly burned, and the *decemvirs* (ten-man councils) performed various rites and sacrifices to assuage the gods.[3] Given that we now know that wasps do not swarm, and given the perennial confusion between wasps and honeybees, it seems more than likely that the Capuans made a simple taxonomic error, and reduced their honeybee colonies by one. The gods were probably rolling their eyes in despair.

At the parochial end of the prophesy scale, wasps and hornets were also claimed to foretell the weather. According to Edward Topsell:

> If they flie about in greater numbers, and be oftener seen about any place, then usually they are wont, it is a signe of heat and fair weather the next day. But if about twilight they are observed to enter their nests, as though they would hide themselves, you must the next day expect rain, winde, or some stormy, troublesome or boysterous season.[4]

According to Rev. J. G. Wood in his *Nature's Teachings* (1907), wasps ably demonstrate how the Creator had wasps anticipate paper-making long before humans.

Like so many omens, the signs are circular – wasps, hornets (and bees) thrive in hot dry weather and in summer, when they are active, the chances are that one fine wasp-favouring sunny day will be followed by another.

To try and get back on track, the scientist has to argue for a genuine ecological place in the world for wasps. It's actually very easy.

NEARLY THE TOP OF THE FOOD CHAIN

Wasps are amongst the most important insect predators after birds and spiders. Wasp predation on other insects is difficult to quantify, but even back-of-the-envelope calculations are quite impressive. If a nest produces 10,000 wasps over a season (quite a conservative estimate), then that means 10,000 grubs, each requiring several meals a day of captured and partly chewed insect prey. A mature colony of wasps is reckoned to collect 3,000–4,000 prey items a day at the height of the season.[5] Hoverflies, house flies, caterpillars, aphids and spiders are favourite food items, but they will also attack butterflies (cutting off the wings and leaving them behind), honeybees (as decried by bee-keepers in New Zealand and elsewhere), small dragonflies, beetles, earwigs, plant bugs, ants, midges, mosquitoes and woodlice. Whatever they can get really.

Prey type is not the key factor so much as prey weight – 8.5 mg per wasp in Britain, but only 6.9 mg for some reason in France.[6] The massive Japanese hornet *Vespa orientalis* can carry up to 500 mg.[7] That's very nearly an entire hawkmoth caterpillar. A quick bit of extrapolation in New Zealand calculated 75,000 prey items per hectare (2.5 ac) per season.[8] This compares very favourably with calculations made to show how helpful some common songbirds are at eating 25,000 grasshoppers per hectare

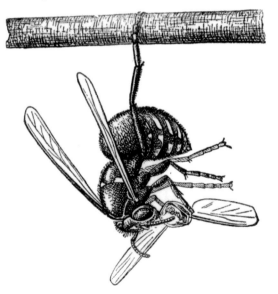

Having caught its fly, a wasp hangs about in the undergrowth with its snack.

per year. A widely touted internet estimate suggests that social wasps across the UK take 14,000 tonnes of insect prey across the summer. These are truly significant volumes of insects consumed.

Taking whatever prey is available is one of the cornerstones of population control and ecological balance. In one of the first monographs dedicated to social wasp study, Edward Latham Ormerod refers to a farmer who carefully destroyed all the wasp nests on his estate and who was rewarded by a plague of flies two years later.[9] This shows the dangers of interfering with nature, and natural balance – it's called karma.

If a particular insect is suddenly very successful and numbers escalate, predators (in this case wasps) will come across it more often and more frequently take it as prey, thus bringing numbers

Built in the open, attached to a plant stem by a single narrow stalk, and being small and compact means that *Polistes* wasp nests can easily be removed and translocated (or destroyed).

Waiting on a fresh horse dropping, a *Mellinus* wasp pounces on incoming bluebottles and other faeces-feeding flies. This is a 'solitary' species, but yellow-jackets also regularly hunt around animal scats.

down again. This density-dependent hunting strategy was put to use in the cotton fields of the Caribbean islands of St Vincent and St Kitts a hundred years ago, when *Polistes* paper wasps were encouraged to nest around the field edges to control cotton leaf-worm (caterpillars of a drab brown moth, *Alabama argillacea*) which was devastating the crops.[10] The small, easily moveable umbrella-shaped combs of the paper wasps perfectly lend themselves to this sort of biological control. A similar wasp species, *Ropalidia gregaria*, was similarly transported around the sugar cane fields of the Philippines where they helped reduce numbers of sap-sucking leaf-hoppers.[11]

Wasps are voracious predators, and if bee-keepers can turn a blind eye to a few losses outside their hives, they offer a useful service in forest, farm and garden. The writer Laurie Lee perfectly described 'jazzing wasps' in *Cider with Rosie* (1959) as they strut around a fallen apple: 'the walzing wasp consumes his share'. The jerking dance is not, though, the accompaniment to an easy and casual meal, and although some fruit is definitely eaten, the hunting continues. Wasps have often been observed apparently deliberately waiting at a holed apple and pouncing on the many flies that also come to drink the fermenting juices. They also hunt around animal droppings, snatching at dung flies and dung beetles attracted to the ripe offering.[12]

The accumulating biomass of wasps in the nest is not a one-way process. Apart from the hungry attentions of badger, ratel and honey buzzard devouring the maggot brood, adult wasps are themselves subject to being eaten, mostly by birds. The *New Scientist*'s reader questions-and-answers column, 'Last Word', gave rise to a series of books, the first of which, *Does Anything Eat Wasps?* (2005), played on the apparently intriguing answer that yes, actually, lots of things eat wasps.[13] Despite their tail-tip weapon, wasps regularly fall prey to spiders, and have no defence against the sticky strands of the orb-web silk. Elsewhere, dragonflies, robber flies, mantids, frogs and crabs have all been recorded catching and eating adult wasps. Fish, too, will gobble down a

Postcard commissioned by the Royal Medical and Chirurgical Society in December 1895. Frogs will eat wasps but are unlikely to share their captures thus. The wasp is labelled mycelium, referring to the hair-like roots of fungi, but the joke is now lost.

wasp struggling on the water's surface, hence a wide range of very realistic wasp fishing flies is available from angling shops.

Tales of various mammals eating wasps are normally referring to those feeding on the brood combs. In North America, racoons, skunks and wolverines are regulars. Fox reports should be taken with a pinch of salt, though; their muzzles do not have the dense fur necessary to keep the wasps at bay and there are plenty of YouTube videos from night-time camera traps showing foxes attempting to dig out a nest but dancing about in pain before fleeing. In one of Enid Blyton's *Brer Rabbit* retellings, poor old Brer Fox gets tricked into lunging at what he is told is a nice bunch of grapes hanging in a vine; he sees that some wasps have got there first so he decides to wipe them off with his tail. Of course it's an aerial yellow-jacket nest and they sting him until he squeals. Three hundred years earlier Edward Topsell reported something

Wasps are ferocious predators of other insects, but themselves fall victim to hunters; in this case the wasp sting was no use against the superior silk-spinning tactics of the common garden spider, *Araneus diadematus*.

Wasps feeding on the remains of a dead rat; not the sort of thing you want walking over your cream tea later in the day.

slightly different: 'Raynard the Fox . . . wily thief thrusteth his bushy tail into the wasps nest, there holding it so long until he perceive it to be full of them, then drawing it slily forth, he beateth and smiteth his tail full of wasps against the next stone or tree, never resting so long as he seeth any of them alive.'[14] Unlikely as it seems, Ms Blyton's grasp of fox and wasp ecology is here nearer to the truth.

Insectivorous birds have only a split second to make the final swooping kill. Nevertheless nearly 150 bird species have been seen feeding on live wasps. Specialist 'bee-eaters' and shrikes mostly take wasps (but will also accept bees), which they catch in the air, then brush against the ground or a tree branch to disembowel the sting or at least evacuate the venom sac. But plenty of common garden birds like blackbirds, great tits, jays and swifts also eat wasps.

Social wasps regularly visit carrion and chew off small morsels of flesh – as far as they're concerned it's all useful protein for their grubs. So clearing up and recycling putrescent remains could be added to their list of helpful purposes on Earth. This does sometimes bring them into conflict with humans because the wasps are unable to tell readily available free roadside carrion from the protected displays in the butcher's or fishmonger's shop. A word of warning here, should wasps come visiting the cream tea: though there is no need to flap pathetically at them, thus enraging them, wasps should not be encouraged to walk across food since they might have visited a rotting corpse earlier in the day and still be carrying untold numbers of nasty bacteria on their feet.

POLLINATION SERVICES

Bees, thanks to the huge propaganda machinery of the honey industry, have almost fully cornered the pollination recognition award system. Hoverflies are sometimes grudgingly acknowledged, along with a few moths, butterflies and beetles. This, of course, does a great disservice to wasps who also visit a large number of flowers after nectar. These include garden and wild species, herbs, shrubs and trees. The trouble is that these waspish attentions are sometimes misrepresented. It is not clear whether Christina Rossetti was praising or denigrating when, in 'The Goblin Market' (1862), she likened her protagonist Lizzie to 'a fruit-crown'd orange-tree, / White with blossoms honey-sweet / Sore beset by wasp and bee'.[15] It sounds more like the bees and wasps are attacking the orange flowers rather than helping create the next harvest of fruits. At least bees and wasps are lumped together rather than the bees alone being applauded.

Although they visit many plant species, social wasps are specialist visitors at figwort flowers, which are rather shallow and suit their short tongues, and also plants like hogweed and ivy, which have exposed nectaries. They are also the primary pollinators of helleborines. These are an elegant but sporadic group of tall and attractive temperate orchids. Despite a large nectar reward they are almost exclusively visited by vespine wasps and are ignored by bees and hoverflies. The flowers attract the wasps by emitting a series of volatile scents; but instead of flowery perfumes, these complex chemicals are similar to those given off by damaged leaves. The assumption is that the predatory wasps are drawn to similar scents from plants whose leaves are genuinely under attack from, say, caterpillars. Called kairomones, these damage scents

The wasp on this German postcard, c. 1950, is more a decorative flourish rather than a true depiction of a pollinator.

Male of *Dolichovespula norwegica* feeding at a helleborine flower. The white lumps on the wasp's face are pollinia, clumped pollen masses that get glued to the head as it drinks the nectar.

are sometimes likened to 'help-me' calls from the plant under attack, summoning the predatory wasps to cart off the offending caterpillars. When they arrive on the helleborine flowers, wasps become drowsy, slowed by some soporific effect in the nectar. This makes them linger, all the better to pick up the pollen, which will be transferred when they are attracted to another helleborine shortly.

PHARMACEUTICAL EXPERIMENTATION

Entomologists lag behind botanists when it comes to exploring pharmacologically active compounds. The 'point' of plants has always been a mixed bag – some are eaten, some are pretty and others provide flavouring and medicinal or recreational herbs. Animals, on the other hand have had to supply meat, fur, draught or companionship to qualify as useful. Most insects fall outside this arc of meritocracy. Things may be about to change for wasps.

Despite the lack of an easy antidote to wasp stings, or possibly because of it, there is a compelling fascination with the physical effects of a sting. Like so many other dangerous chemicals, wasp venom is now being considered for its potential medicinal uses. It has been examined for promising use as antibiotic and as 'magic bullet' mechanism to attack targeted cells in the body. Mastoparan, a key constituent of wasp venom, is able to latch onto certain lipid (fatty acid) types in the cell membranes of a target organ, creating a portal into that specific body cell type.[16] Moving medical chemicals around the body, whether injected directly into the bloodstream or swallowed, has often been difficult. The chemical may only be needed in one part of the body, or one organ, but gets shunted around in the bloodstream everywhere, causing harm in some places as well as help in others. If the wasp venom, or a synthesized variant of it, can be chemically targeted to one particular type of body cell, any pharmaceutical attached to it gets targeted too.

The latest iteration is the possibility that a component from the venom of the large black Brazilian social wasp *Polybia paulista* can disrupt and kill cancerous tumour cells;[17] at least it does this in test mice studies by latching onto the faulty tumour cells, which have different membrane lipids, thus rupturing and destroying them.

Some recent work has suggested that wasp and bee venoms, or their components, might have a use in treating neurodegenerative diseases like Alzheimer's, Parkinson's, multiple sclerosis and epilepsy, but these are still early days.[18] There is already a lively market in harvested wasp venoms, but so far these products have mostly been used to test allergic reactions to the venom itself, to warn of the potential for anaphylaxis in susceptible victims in the future.

There was a time when wasps formed part of a broad pharmacopoeia, often combined with supernatural beliefs in their spiritual power that was verging on magic. Pliny the Elder seemed to believe that a wasp, caught with the left hand then tied or fastened to any part of the body, was a good defence against quartan ague – one of the lesser forms of malaria. Crushing a wasp into distilled water was held to have great virtue, as was a similar ointment made of wasps crushed into vinegar, oil, or cow dung as an antidote to wasp stings. Care was needed though. According to the physician Mizaldus (or sometimes Mizault), any part of the body to be therewith anointed

> it straight ways causeth it to swell monstrously, and to be puffed up, that you would imagine them to be sick with the dropsie [oedema]: and this course crafty drabs and queans use to perswade their sweet hearts, that they are forsooth with childe by them: thus many times beguiling and blinding the eyes of wary and expert midwives.[19]

It seems unlikely that any part of a wasp was ever included in the yellow-jackets laxatives manufactured by Bristol, Myers & Company in the early twentieth century: 'As a laxative one at night. As a cathartic dose one or two night and morning,' according to the bottle. Quite what the company was trying to do is now unclear. Though the company found early fortune in its *sal hepatica* laxative (a dry mix of salts including sodium sulphate, baking soda, tartaric acid and common cooking salt), there seems a fine line between this and marketing wasp venom and snake oil, which by that time had already become the standard name for the archetypal medical hoax. This, however, has not stopped wasps being routinely misappropriated for marketing and hype.

Just because wasps have painful stings, it does not mean that they are necessarily shunned or associations with them discouraged. In fact the opposite can be the case because the brand is all about the subliminal messages passing through society – sometimes those 'bad' feelings about wasps can be good for sales. That Wasp airgun pellets sting is a good thing; that's what they're meant to do. Likewise Remington .22 Yellow Jacket bullets and Wasp Archery products would be expected to hurt like hell. Yellow-jackets are no longer associated with constipation, but perhaps a stinging punch is delivered by the energy pills containing ephedrine and caffeine now marketed under that name. Wasp brand tattoo needles almost certainly sting, and perhaps the Wasp brand vaping vaporizer delivers a kick.

Waspishness is more, though, than just looking cool and actually stinging. It's also to do with being thrilled and excited. Vespa scooters, the iconic, chic Italian motorcycle, don't look or feel like hornets, but maybe their high-pitched engines are enough to give a jolt of nervous energy – a buzz. Maybe Wasp high performance motor suspension products offer the same? Likewise Wasp switches, Wasp fuel systems and Wasp Logger Software maybe all give that frisson of tense excitement.

Part of the wasp brand is an air of menace, anger or threat. Why else would there have been nine British warships (and a shore establishment) called HMS *Wasp* between 1749 and 1886? The USS *Wasp* launched in 1987 is now the archetype for the wasp class of aircraft carriers, and is the tenth menacing U.S. navy ship to bear

Clever winged wasp/scooter mash-up for an enamel lapel pin produced for Piaggio Vespa scooter enthusiasts.

the name. It is perhaps coincidental that WASP (an acronym for World Aquanaut Security Patrol) was the secret quasi-military organization hosting *Stingray*, the 1960s children's sci-fi marionette TV series about the adventures of a high-tech submarine. There is nothing remotely marine about wasps, but the logo used on-screen and in merchandizing incorporated this unlikely insect with the usual suspicious number of wings and legs. The Westland Wasp anti-submarine helicopter, the Wasp air-to-ground missile, a Wasp torpedo boat and various Wasp aeroplane engines maintain the insect's edgy reputation in military circles.

There are also wasp sports kits, although this may be more to do with narrow waists shown off by tight-fitting Lycra (and the logo looks confusingly bumblebee-like). Wasp hockey products are a bit puzzling – apart from black and yellow hockey shoes it's difficult to see what the link is. The logo is a stylized wasp face rather than the usual twisting pointed sting-tipped abdomen; although this may be distinctive enough to the hymenopterist it is probably lost on the non-entomological hockey-playing fraternity.

This film poster from 1914 does not even need to show a wasp for its *Blue Flame* series detective dramas.

There is also quite some latitude with wasp symbolism in the international music industry. On the one hand there is a Spanish heavy metal recording label called Avispa; on the other, in 1972 French free-jazz trumpeter Bernard Vitet released his *La Guêpe* album of interesting, if challenging, melody-free compositions. The U.S. jazz-fusion quartet Yellowjackets is somewhere in between.

The wasp brand and logo is not a new phenomenon. Putting aside those ancient Egyptian hieroglyphs which may be wasps but could quite easily be honeybees, the earliest stylized symbols probably appeared on coats of arms. The powerful Barberini family of Rome originally had three wasps on their family shield, but between 1604 and 1607 Maffeo Barberini, then head of the family and papal nuncio to Henry IV's court in Paris, redesigned the coat of arms and replaced the wasps with bees.[20] In 1623 he went on to become Pope Urban VIII; perhaps the biblical industry and valuable productivity of bees was seen as a better role model than the waspish aggression that had served his ancestors. Sadly most other potential 'wasp' depictions in coats of arms turn out to be nondescript insect-type things, becoming laughably incorrect in modern reinterpretations. The Italian Vespucci family (close-enough sounding to *Vespa* to be of interest) have a shield variously depicted as being red with a blue diagonal bar overlaid with a line of gold insects which might or might not be wasps, but one modern representation clearly shows horntails – this large black-and-yellow insect with a stout and menacing (but non-stinging) egg-laying tube at the end of its tail is only distantly

Hornets make superb decorative motifs, in this case on a jumper in the Cowichan (Vancouver Island First Nations) style.

related to wasps. The three common wasps on the badge of La Vespière, a village in the Calvados region of northern France, is a modern fabrication, dating only from 2013, so hardly counts.

According to the College of Arms in London, the official heraldic authority for England, Wales, Northern Ireland and much of the Commonwealth, the hornet might appear in one coat. An application made to the College found a description of the arms of the Bollard family as 'sable a hornet argent' (a silver hornet on a black shield).[21] However, the present Richmond Herald, one of the formal officers of the College, was sceptical since the drawing is so simple and could easily be a bee. He did, however, offer to assist in the design of a new crest should the success of this book warrant the author's taking an exulted wasp-themed coat of arms in the near future. Perhaps this might be added to the personalized number plate that popped up on Facebook Marketplace during early research – W13SPS.

8 Past Perceptions and Future Prospects

Throughout history there has been an uneasy tension between those studying wasps – natural philosophers, naturalists, entomologists, hymenopterists – and a general public generally ignorant of wasps but sometimes at the receiving end of their stings. This disparity between observed facts and superstitious folklore has morphed into a contest between scientific knowledge and tabloid inanity. Science keeps progressing, knowledge is accruing, understanding has deepened over time, but wasps are still misunderstood. How have we got here?

Taking Aristotle's baseline of good-mother, dronish, sting-or-not half truths, not much changed in wasp reportage for 1,800 years. By the time of the *Hortus Sanitatis* (1491), it was widely known that wasps were predators that cut the heads and wings off flies, and were also carrion visitors, but the author is still touting the nonsense that they 'growe out of roten fowle horse flesche'.[1] The myth that 27 hornet stings will kill a child also gets yet another airing.

Despite their inappropriate leg number, wasps and hornets are included (ten pages of them) in just about the first English zoology texts – Edward Topsell's *History of Four-footed Beasts* (1607) and *History of Serpents* (1608). According to the conventions of the time they were included in the serpent section along with a few other 'insects' such as spiders and scorpions. As noted earlier,

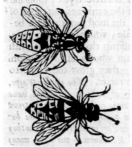

Illustrations of 'wasps' from Thomas Muffet's *Theatre of Insects* (1658). The triplet on the right are almost certainly not wasps, the largest clearly the hornet robberfly, *Asilus crabroniformis*.

Thomas Muffet wrote the first book about insects in English, finally published in 1658 when it was issued with a combined Topsell beasts-and-serpents omnibus.[2] Muffet's nine pages on wasps and hornets (now with some woodcuts too) are remarkably similar to Topsell's, down to the same anecdotes about sparrow-killing hornet attacks. Yet this exemplifies the writing of the age. In fact both authors raided the works of others wholesale, from the received wisdom of the ancients to their own recently published contemporaries. Cutting and pasting is by no means a new phenomenon, and there seemed little difference between plagiarism and homage.

Both books stand at a watershed of scientific learning and publishing. They both offer the standard wisdom of Aristotle, Pliny and all the other revered writers from before the Dark Ages, but they also include a few novel personal observations. It may not always be possible to detect who is genuinely doing the observing, but some truths ring true amongst the confused buzzing of myth, superstition and often garbled fallacy. The modern scientific world of the Renaissance was about to take over.

The main instrument of any modern entomologist is the microscope, and the development of the first simple optical devices in
the seventeenth century led to the publication of extraordinary
observations by Anton van Leeuwenhoek and Robert Hooke.
Hooke's *Micrographia* (1665) has some spectacular pictures of
fleas, head lice, ants, fly feet and a bee sting, but he does not con-
sider wasps other than to wonder why bluebottles buzz like them.[3]
Thankfully this was put right by supremely competent Dutch
scientist Jan Swammerdam (1637–1680).

Swammerdam was working down his microscope in the
Netherlands in the 1660s and '70s, and although he published
some results in 1669, his main work *The Book of Nature* was not
published until 1737–8, nearly sixty years after his death, with an
English translation in 1758.[4] Swammerdam took Hooke's close-up
observations further by giving detailed descriptions and offering
excellent biological explanations of what he saw. He is best
known to hymenopterists for his exquisite dissections of bees
(and wasps also) and for finally working out that queens were
female (he counted about 5,100 eggs in the paired ovaries of one
specimen) and that drones were male. Finally the good mother
was confirmed.

He was initially uncertain about the worker bees and wasps,
but knew they manifestly were not the dangerously armed warrior males so often alluded to by classical writers. We can get
some idea that he fully appreciated the significance of his own
findings by his exultation in print:

Behold! these are the entrails of the common or working
bee; there does not appear among them the smallest trace
of spermatic organs or the genital parts, or of any thing

which can answer the purpose of, or be compared to a penis or ovary. Hence I think these bees may most justly and properly be said to be natural eunuchs, and such can only work and feed, cherish and rear the progeny of others as their own. On the contrary, as I have beforementioned, the genital organs are very plainly seen in the drones, as they are the true males of the bees; their whole belly is in a manner filled with testicles.

Later he reiterates that the workers are, indeed, females like the queen, but sterile:

the common bees have no ovary, and therefore, like women who have lived virgins till they are past child-bearing, serve only the purpose of labour in the oeconomy of the whole body. These are thus by nature rendered incapable of doing any other business but that of nourishing and educating the young offspring.[5]

This idea of eunuch (metaphorically at least) female worker bees and wasps lived on for two centuries in the common use of 'neuter' to describe them, and the Hymenoptera have a special symbol (☿, also astrological Mercury) to denote workers, in addition to those used everywhere else for male (♂, Mars) and female (♀, Venus). Nowadays modern texts contain the same symbols, but refer to workers as sterile, non-functional, non-reproductive, subordinate or non-gyne females. Some workers' abdomens do contain functional ovaries, but because they cannot mate, they can only lay unfertilized, haploid eggs which can only develop into males.

Swammerdam's useful observations of wasps and hornets show that he tried to work out how many times a brood cell was used by counting the exuviae (cast skins) of the larvae; he dissected

Muffet's hornets are perhaps the best portrayed of his wasps.

hornet grubs in the combs and observed how they produce silk thread from a gland at their mouthparts to cover over the cell when they are fully fed, ready for metamorphosis into the adult stage.[6] Swammerdam also extended previous observations on bee and wasp stings, by dissecting those from hornets which were larger and thus easier to manipulate. He showed that it was not the sting spike itself, nor the mechanism of the two barbed lancets that caused the pain: 'nor does its puncture hurt more than that of a needle. For experiment's sake I have often wounded myself with the sting, and felt no other ill consequence from it than a slight itching in the wounded part.' He did, however, also experiment on himself with venom that he squeezed from the muscular poison reservoir: 'This, as soon as it drops into the wound, produces the pain.'

Swammerdam's illustrations of adult wasps, hornets and other Hymenoptera are superb, and generally identifiable to modern species. He depicts the small umbrella nest of a paper wasp (though upside down, suggesting it was brought to him rather than finding it himself) and a small carton nest, but it is clear that his gaze was directed at the insects themselves and into their bodily interiors, rather than at their nests. He was clearly in awe of his diminutive subjects.

The first major publication dedicated wholly to wasps is 'Histoire des Guespes' by the great French naturalist René Réaumur (1683–1757). His 47-page essay, complete with engraved plates of wasps, larvae and nests of several species, does not yet include modern scientific names, and Aristotle and Pliny still get namechecks, but the descriptions, and engravings, of cell and comb (*gateau*) construction, hibernating queens and sting mechanisms are based on first-hand personal observation rather than repeated reinterpretation of 2,000-year-old commentaries.[7] His careful descriptions and observations on nest carton construction offer perhaps the first detailed report on the fact that wasps create their own paper from chewed wood pulp; he is credited with transforming the French paper-making industry from relying on rags and hemp to using wood pulp.

NAMES MATTER

Carl Linnaeus (Carl von Linné, 1707–1778) was not particularly interested in wasps – he was primarily a botanist – but his idea to give formal international scientific names to all plants and animals revolutionized how we see the natural world. Where previously writers like Topsell and Muffet had been limited to talking about large wasps and small wasps, hornets of the 'yellow kinde', and the wood or 'wilde' hornet, often mixing together half-understood names from ancient Greece and Rome, Linnaeus crystallized many previous disorganized schemes, gathered all known creatures into coherent groups and started to give them two names – genus and species. The common wasp became *Vespa vulgaris*, the hornet *Vespa crabro*, the honeybee *Apis mellifera*. This was more than just taking old names and giving them shiny new ones; the old names frequently reflected an Old Testament world where creatures were defined by scripture (religious or classical) and were barely understood except in terms of whether they had cloven hooves, were an abomination for going on more than four feet and whether they could be eaten on the Sabbath. The new scientific approach to nature was not trying to understand how it could be shoe-horned into some preordained doctrine, but trying to understand it by observing it afresh – looking at it closely, examining real physical differences between different animals, and more importantly describing them with sufficient clarity that someone else would be able to understand it. Linnaeus gave a focus, a starting point, from which the naming and understanding of relatedness and classification could spread.

Linnaeus published his first catalogue of named plants and animals, his *Systema Naturae* in 1735, and he kept adding and changing things with each new edition. To fix that focus in time, modern biologists take his major enlarged and overhauled tenth edition, published in 1758, as the starting point for current biological nomenclature, and all modern scientific names are built on that zero-hour foundation.[8]

Trying to understand what Muffet meant by the pseudospheca (literally 'false wasp'), 'a kind of wasp having no sting . . . short horns . . . great eyes . . . long forked mouth . . . two dusky coloured

The European hornet, which still retains Linnaeus' original scientific name, *Vespa crabro*. This is a male, with the slightly longer, down-curved antennae.

wings' was taxing to start with. Judging from the picture that illustrates his paragraph it wasn't a wasp anyway, but the wasp-mimic robber fly called by Linnaeus *Asilus crabroniformis*. It is still called that today. Rather than try and decode what the ancients were calling things, Linnaeus started again and his method spread out across the civilized world as others took up his lead and ran with it. As 'new' species were discovered they were given new names, but always adhering to that binomial genus/species name pair, and increasingly arranged in sensible scientifically justifiable generic or family groupings and thence into orders and classes. In his revision of Swedish wasp species in 1869, Carl G. Thomson coined the diminutive *Vespula* for the slightly smaller social wasps, leaving the larger species (hornets) in the genus *Vespa*.[9] Sievert A. Rohwer later invented *Dolichovespula* for the delicate long-faced species that make the aerial tree-hanging nests that are so easy to bump into in comic strips, including that pesky European invader *Dolichovespula media*.[10]

Not everything proceeded in an orderly and scientifically solemn manner, though. As was noted earlier, Linnaeus' Danish

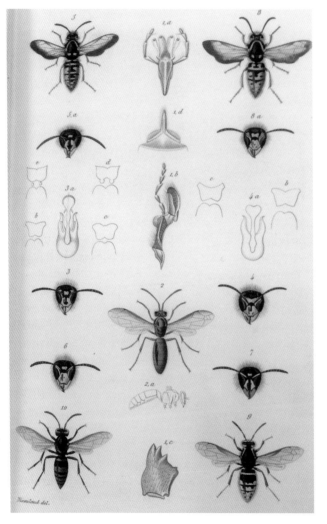

Colour plate from a wasp monograph by Saussure, featuring (bottom left) *Vespula bellicosa.*

pupil Fabricius set a tabloid headline tripwire-in-waiting when he named his geographically suspect new species *espula germanica*. French entomologist Henri de Saussure must have realized he might be playing to a less-informed audience when, in 1854, he named a new wasp *Vespula bellicosa*.[11] Thankfully the bellicose wasp does not occur in the British Isles.

Deciphering pre-Linnaean names can be a battle of stretched logic beyond comprehension, but on this side of that zero hour the comparisons are relatively easy and corrections and alterations can be made without upset. Things continue to change, but only in the framework of a stable and cohesive taxonomy. It's bad enough that gall wasps and fairy wasps are still called 'wasps' in English today; they have little connection to yellow-jackets, but when using their scientific names they are the families Cynipidae and Mymaridae and are obviously separated by many millions of evolutionary years and by more than a chapter or two in Hymenoptera monographs.

We now know what we are talking about, and can communicate across continents rather than having to guess from some vague description what an entomologist in another country, speaking another language, is on about. Not everyone is following this new system though. Journalists, in particular, are suspicious of scientific names and constantly worry that using them will alienate their readers – it will not. Tabloid features today are still flailing about with an Aristotelian name system where 'wasp' can mean anything from a gold-and-black-barred yellow-jacket social wasp, to a tiny ant-like creature making plant galls, to virtually any slim, sharp-tailed stinging insect. We have come so far, but we are still so far behind.

The first book in English dedicated to the social wasps was that by Edward Latham Ormerod in 1868.[12] Measured, logically reasonable and highly scientific in its content, its tone set the standard for all modern wasp books. Although many new observations have been made since, his descriptions are first class, as are his black-and-white lithographs of various wasp nests and his delicately hand-painted engravings of the insects themselves.

Throughout, he proposes calm observation and experimentation with wasps, and was one of the first advocates of paint-marking captured and released (and recaptured) insects to monitor their numbers and behaviour. To this end he also describes the first known precursor of the pooter. This strange contraption, used for sucking up small insects unharmed into a glass collecting bottle is widely known but poorly understood by bemused non-entomologists.

> I prefer a glass tube, about twelve inches long by three-eighths of an inch wide. This should be joined, by a piece of India-rubber tubing, to a mouth-piece, and be stopped at this end by a few turns of fine wire, loosely packed, so as to let the air pass freely, but to catch the wasp as it is drawn in. With this instrument, with a little practice, any wasp, even the sentinel herself, may be picked up without causing a commotion. Once within the draught of the tube, the wasp flies up to the stop in a moment. It remains only to blow her down very gently, and catch her in gloved fingers.[13]

This was groundbreaking stuff. Ormerod confines himself to sober observations and only very briefly goes into details of how to get rid of nests, or control pest numbers. He does, however, give detailed instructions for excavating nests for the purposes of scientific examination: 'all more or less exciting, dirty and dangerous'. Throughout he is practical and objective, recommending a suit of fustian and bee veils whenever in close proximity to a nest, and suggesting that old favourite crushed mallow leaves as the approved remedy for stings, or if the pain is extreme then ammonia, soda or, at a pinch, chloroform. About the only time he departs from his staid style is to relate the tale of an Uckfield

Wasps (although these look like hornets) and nest, from the celebratory *The Insect* by Jules Michelet (1875), originally published in French. According to the author, wasps go 'zou, zou, zou'. Lovely.

butcher who revenged himself on the wasps that stole morsels of meat from his counter displays.

> Long practice, with a sharp pair of scissors, had made him so dexterous that he could snip off a wing without interrupting the wasp at her work. When the wasp had cut off a piece of meat she tried to fly away with it, but finding she could not fly, thought the piece was too large to carry, and cut it in half, and so she went on cutting the meat smaller and smaller.[14]

Wasps, it seems are intelligent creatures, capable of calculating payloads and their own aerial thrust vectors, but it still appears acceptable to torment and torture them.

If Mr Ormerod was happy to leave wasps and merely observe and comment on them, his sister Eleanor Anne Ormerod took a different tack. As Consultant Economic Entomologist to the Royal Agricultural Society, she collected data and published widely on various garden, farm and forestry pests. In her earlier work on injurious insects of 1890, she made no mention of wasps as being considered a nuisance, either in the garden or in the farmer's field, but she includes a detailed chapter in her 1898 book on the pests of orchard and bush fruits.[15] This, she admits, is because five years earlier she had witnessed the huge wasp depredations to fruit-growers during the 'wasp plague'. Her remedies include destroying and digging out wasp nests, usually by pouring tar, cyanide of potassium, sulphur mixture, paraffin, gun powder or any mixture thereof down into the nest entrance. In that plague year of 1893, a bounty of sixpence per nest was paid for 376 nests within a mile of a Sussex kitchen garden. She does not relate whether or not this was rewarded in the following years by plagues of flies.

Every year, towards the end of summer, wasps start to make up a high proportion of the insects flying around in parks and gardens or along the hedgerow, as numbers of workers in the nest burgeon. They go about their business of collecting prey items for their grubs back in the increasing carton nest. The numbers of bees also increase. For the usual reasons the one population is decried and oppressed, the other is lauded and celebrated.

The recent wide concern over broad-spectrum neonicotinoid insecticide sprays has drawn huge scientific and campaigning efforts to bear on the declines of top pollinators, and although bees dominate this scene, other insects are also affected, including wasps. These are all reported in scientific articles, but you'd be hard pressed to know it from media reports, even when the 'bee'

Wasps collect water to spread on to their paper combs, which they then fan with their wings to produce an effective air-conditioning system in the nest. This worker of *Dolichovespula media* was drinking from the flooded leaf axil of a teasel plant, and also eating drowned insects, from which the plant also obtains some nutrients.

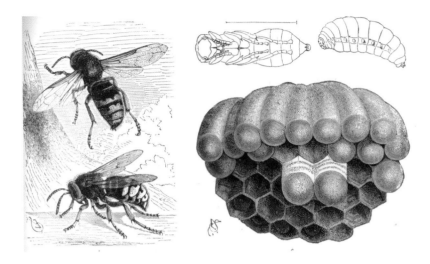

accompanying the story is a wrongly labelled hoverfly or even a wasp. When a recent German study deplored the vanishment of insects in the general countryside during the last fifty years, there was righteous condemnation of humanity's poor stewardship of nature.[16] Headlines bemoaned the loss of butterflies, ladybirds and, of course, bees, but not one flagged up the concomitant loss of wasps.

And yet wasps are actually incredibly useful study tools when looking at the health of the countryside. Social and solitary wasps are key indicators of habitat quality and conservation effort.[17] Their specialist habitat requirements, often combined with their preference for warm, dry, sunny nesting sites and varied availability of insect prey, allows them to be monitors of biodiversity and environmental stability. A diverse species make-up is a good sign of a diverse mosaic of microhabitats at a site, a particularly important yardstick for vulnerable localities on limestone hills, sandy heaths and maritime undercliffs. A healthy wasp community

The life history of the hornet, courtesy of the enthusiastically uplifting text of *The Royal Natural History* written by Richard Lydekker (1896).

A hornet larva scrabbling in the remains of its nest, which has been destroyed by some well-meaning but misguided person who could only see peril in a hornet nest in London's Dulwich Park.

is a sign of a healthy countryside. The Big Wasp Survey aims to get baseline data in place for the social wasps, now that their responsible-sampling/mass-murder public relations faux pas has been addressed. This large citizen science project laudably aims to involve members of the general public, rather than just the usual specialist entomologists, and its media message is that these insects are important and useful for understanding and monitoring the natural world. Let's hope the media will understand the wasp names presented to them. The large numbers of social wasps at the end of the summer make them keystone species – they are numerous enough to make them ecologically significant in almost any terrestrial food web, and larger or smaller numbers of them in any given year will have knock-on effects on other organisms – their predators and their prey.

Wasp study also gives us a tool for understanding long-term changes coming to the world. The appearance of *Dolichovespula media* in Britain, and its less newsworthy Saxon congener *Dolichovespula saxonica*, demonstrate how organisms colonize and disseminate across a new environment, and lessons from studying their geographic spreads will be all the more important as climate change alters the landscape. Many more creatures will expand or contract their ranges with the new climatic conditions, and studying warmth-loving wasps offers useful models of what may or may not happen in the next crucial decades.

Wasps could also lead the way in promoting nature conservation and an appreciation of wildlife in general. At the top of the wasp size hierarchy, the European hornet, *Vespa crabro*, is well placed to mirror the red kite, peregrine falcon and other impressive

Ready to take up the reins of wasp appreciation: a worker hornet, a handsome and fascinating insect.

birds of prey, the return of which into the open countryside is now celebrated after previous catastrophic declines. Despite their large size and uneasy folk familiarity, hornets have ever been secretive and actually relatively scarce in Britain. They appeared to take a terrible knock in the middle of the twentieth century, probably as a result of agriculture intensification after the Second World War, but since the 1980s they have recovered slightly; they are now spreading to localities previously unknown to them, including urban central London, East Sussex, Kent, the Isle of Man and recently northern Scotland.[18] This may have to do with changes in rural woodland management as well as in climate. An active recording scheme organized by the inclusively titled Bees, Wasps and Ants Recording Society continues to monitor these and other wasp species throughout the country.

There is already a precedent for improved wasp and hornet appreciation. In Britain, the stag beetle *Lucanus cervus* is now a flagship conservation species bringing awareness to the vulnerability of its declining and threatened habitats, and awe-inspired wonder at its huge size and somewhat menacing form. The hornet is ideally poised to be its vespine equivalent. But in order for this to happen, humans need to appreciate it for what it is – not the demonic stinging fiend that is sometimes portrayed, but a striking and handsome wasp with a fascinating life history and curious behaviour, a natural denizen of Britain's verdant woodlands. Can we put aside our fears? Can we find environmental knowledge and worldly wisdom in a misunderstood and wrongly persecuted insect? Now is the time to take a stand with the wasps. The truth is out there, but to deliver it the wasps need all the help they can get.

Timeline of the Wasp

175–200 MYA	30 MYA	c. 3000 BC	2641 BC
DNA-calculated common ancestor of all wasps, bees and ants – the stinging Aculeata	Ealiest known fossil social wasp, *Palaoevespula baltica*, discovered in Baltic amber	Ancient Egyptian hieroglyphs may show wasps, or hornets, but most likely honeybees	Ancient Egyptian King Menes supposedly dies of a single hornet sting; more likely a hippopotamus attack

1609	1658	1668	1719
Charles Butler's *The Feminine Monarchie* first proposes that wasp and bee colonies are under control of an overarching alpha female	First major contributions to wasps in English appear in Edward Topsell's *History of Four-footed Beasts and Serpents*, which is also issued with an appendix containing Thomas Muffet's *Theatre of Insects*	Jan Swammerdam uses a microscope to dissect bees, wasps and hornets, and finally confirms that the 'leaders' are female queens rather than kingly males, and that the sting pain comes from the liquid venom	First publication dedicated solely to wasps, 'Histoire des Guespes', an essay by René Réaumur, published in France

1885	1913		1945
Vincent Holt's *Why Not Eat Insects?* contains a recipe for wasp grubs baked in the comb, but it fails to achieve wide culinary acceptance	Charles Richet awarded Nobel Prize for Medicine for work on anaphylactic shock; though using Portuguese man-of-war jellyfish venom, this work paved the way for adrenalin treatment of wasp sting anaphylaxis, too		European wasp *Vespula vulgaris* accidentally established in New Zealand, giving rise to giant perennial nests with millions of workers; *Vespula germanica* established 1978

c. 1450 BC	190 BC	*c.* 4TH CENTURY
God sends hornets to drive out Hivites, Canaanites and Hittites during the biblical Exodus	Portentous swarm of wasps destroyed in Italian city Capua; most likely to have been honeybees since wasps don't swarm	Marcus Christian Bishop of Arethusa is martyred by being drenched with honey and suspended in a basket to be stung to death by wasps

1758	1765	1845	1861
Tenth edition of Carolus Linnaeus' *Systema Naturae*, now the internationally accepted start of modern scientific nomenclature, fixing the common wasp as *Vespula vulgaris* and the European hornet as *Vespa crabro*	Jacob Schäffer credited with being first to use wood pulp to make paper; said to have been directly inspired by watching wasps build their nests	Johann Dzierzon first suggests fertilized and unfertilized eggs develop into females and males respectively, later confirmed as haplodiploid explanation of chromosome numbers	Henry Walter Bates suggests harmless insects gain protection by resembling dangerous stinging models – now called Batesian mimicry

1980	1987	2016	2017
The median wasp, *Dolichovespula media* first colonizes the British Isles; its large size causes consternation in the press	The Saxon wasp, *Dolichovespula saxonica*, arrives in Britain too; the media ignore it	Nest of invasive Asian hornet, *Vespa velutina*, found in Gloucestershire. A notorious nuisance of beehives elsewhere in Europe, the colony was eradicated	Citizen science project The Big Wasp Survey launched to record wasp species and numbers around the British Isles

References

1 A STING IN THE TALE

1   John L. Cloudsley-Thompson, *Insects and History* (London, 1976).
2   Ian C. Beavis, *Insects and Other Invertebrates in Classical Antiquity* (Exeter, 1988), pp. 187–95.
3   Ian Gauld and Barry Bolton, eds, *The Hymenoptera* (Oxford, 1989).
4   J. Philip Spradbery, *Wasps* (Washington, 1973); Robin Edwards, ed., *Social Wasps: Their Biology and Control* (East Grinstead, 1980); Michael E. Archer and James Antony Turner, *The Vespoid Wasps* (London, 2014).
5   Edward Topsell, *History of Four-footed Beasts and Serpents* (London, 1658), p. 660.
6   Edward Saunders, *Hymenoptera Aculeata of the British Islands* (London, 1896).
7   A. P. Rasnitsyn, 'Superorder Vespidea Laicharting, 1781', in *History of Insects,* ed. A. P. Rasnitsyn and Donald L. Quick (Dordrecht, 2002).
8   Joseph C. Bequaert, 'On the Generic and Subgeneric Divisions of the Vespinae (Hymenoptera)', *Bulletin of the Brooklyn Entomological Society*, 25 (1930), pp. 59–70.
9   Edward C. Ash, *Ants, Bees and Wasps: Their Lives, Comedies and Tragedies* (London, 1924), p. 119; John Phipps, 'The Vampire Wasps of British Columbia: An Example of Haematophagy by *Vespula* sp', *Bulletin of the Entomological Society of Canada*, 4 (1974), p. 134.
10 Spradbury, *Wasps*, p. 278.
11 Jan Swammerdam, *The Book of Nature; or, The History of Insects: Reduced to Distinct Classes, Confirmed by Particular Instances,*

Displayed in the Anatomical Analysis of Many Species . . . etc.
(London, 1758).

12 Topsell, *History*, p. 658.

13 Quoted by Spradbery, *Wasps*, p. 277.

14 Topsell, *History*, p. 656.

15 Ibid.

16 Jacob Meydenback (publisher), *Hortus Sanitatis* (Mainz, 1491).

17 William Hutton, *Poems; Chiefly Tales* (London, 1804), p. 45.

18 Nejash Abdela and Kula Jilo, 'Bee Venom and its Therapeutic
    Values: A Review', *Advances in Life Science and Technology*, 44
    (2016), pp. 18–22.

19 Justin O. Schmidt, *The Sting of the Wild* (Baltimore, MD, 2016).

20 Richard A. Jones and Calvin J. S. Ure-Jones, *A Natural History
    of Insects in 100 Limericks* (London, 2019).

2 WARNING COLOURS

1 Fritz Müller, 'Ueber die Vortheile der Mimicry bei Schmetterlingen',
   Zoologische Anzeiger, 1 (1878), pp. 54–5.

2 Edward Topsell, *History of Four-footed Beasts and Serpents* (London,
   1658), p. 651.

3 Thomas Muffet, *The Theatre of Insects; or, Lesser Living Creatures as
   Bees, Flies, Caterpillars, Spiders, Worms, and Co., a Most Elaborate
   Work* (London, 1658), p. 921.

4 Henry W. Bates, 'Contributions to an Insect Fauna of the Amazon
   Valley. Lepidoptera: Heliconidae', *Transactions of the Linnean
   Society*, 23 (1861), pp. 495–566.

5 Brigette Howarth, C. Clee and Malcolm Edmunds, 'The Mimicry
   between British Syrphidae (Diptera) and Aculeate Hymenoptera',
   British Journal of Entomology and Natural History, 12 (2000),
   pp. 1–39.

6 *Recuile d'anciennes poésies françaises*, Bibliotèque nationale de
   France, Bibliotèque de l'Arsenal, Paris, BNF Arsenal item code
   3142, folio 266v.

7 Jacob Meydenback (publisher), *Hortus Sanitatis* (Mainz, 1491).

8   Marcel Dicke, 'Insects in Western Art', *American Entomologist*, 46
    (Winter 2000), pp. 228–36.

3 IT'S IN THEIR GENES

1   Michael E. Archer, 'Population Dynamics', in *Social Wasps: Their
    Biology and Control*, ed. Robin Edwards (East Grinstead, 1980),
    pp. 172–207.
2   Ian C. Beavis, *Insects and Other Invertebrates in Classical Antiquity*
    (Exeter, 1988), p. 192.
3   Thomas Muffet, *The Theatre of Insects; or, Lesser Living Creatures as
    Bees, Flies, Caterpillars, Spiders, Worms, and Co., a Most Elaborate
    Work* (London, 1658), p. 923.
4   Edward Topsell, *History of Four-footed Beasts and Serpents*
    (London, 1658), p. 657.
5   Ibid., p. 653.
6   Ibid., p. 659.
7   Owain W. Richards, 'The Mating-habits of Species of *Vespa*
    (Hymen.)', *Proceedings of the Royal Entomological Society of London*,
    Series A, 12 (1937), pp. 27–9.
8   Johann Dzierzon, 'Chodowanie pszczół – Sztuka zrobienica złota,
    nawet z zielska' [Beekeeping – The Art of Making Gold, Even from
    Weeds], *Tygodnik Polski Poswiecony Wloscianom*, 20 (1845).
9   K. C. Schmidt, B. G. Hunt and C. R. Smith, 'Queen, Worker and
    Male Yellowjacket Wasps Receive Different Nutrition During
    Development', *Insectes Sociaux*, 59 (2012), pp. 289–95.
10 Robin Edwards, ed., *Social Wasps: Their Biology and Control*
    (East Grinstead, 1980), pp. 78–9.
11 Thomas H. Johnson, 'Memoranda and Documents: Some Edward
    Taylor Gleanings', *New England Quarterly*, 16 (1943), pp. 280–96.

4 PAPER ARCHITECTURE

1   Christopher Smart, 'Jubilate Agno', Manuscript Eng 719,
    Houghton Library, Harvard University (1759–63).

2 Thomas Wildman, *A Treatise on the Management of Bees* (London, 1770).

3 John Lubbock, *Ants, Bees and Wasps: A Record of Observations on the Habits of the Social Hymenoptera* (London, 1882), p. 315.

4 Ibid., p. 316.

5 Edward Topsell, *History of Four-footed Beasts and Serpents* (London, 1658), p. 652.

6 Robin Edwards, ed., *Social Wasps: Their Biology and Control* (East Grinstead, 1980), p. 49.

7 John G. Wood, *Nature's Teachings: Human Invention Anticipated by Nature* (London, 1907), p. 474.

8 E. Lily Yu, 'The Cartographer Wasps and the Anarchist Bees', *Clarkesworld Magazine*, 55 (2011).

9 Edwards, *Social Wasps*, p. 53.

10 Thomas Muffet, *The Theatre of Insects; or, Lesser Living Creatures as Bees, Flies, Caterpillars, Spiders, Worms, and Co., a Most Elaborate Work* (London, 1658), p. 922.

11 Edwards, *Social Wasps*, p. 56.

12 B. Kay Clapperton, H. Moller and G. R. Sandlant, 'Distribution of Social Wasps (Hymenoptera: Vespidae) in New Zealand in 1987', *New Zealand Journal of Zoology*, 16 (1989), pp. 315–23.

13 C. R. Thomas, 'The European Wasp (*Vespula germanica* Fab.) in New Zealand', *New Zealand Department of Science and Industry Research Information Series*, 27 (1960), pp. 1–74.

14 Lee A. Dugatkin, 'Inclusive Fitness Theory from Darwin to Hamilton', *Genetics*, 176 (2007), pp. 1375–80.

15 Edwards, *Social Wasps*, p. 13.

16 Vincent Holt, *Why Not Eat Insects?* (London, 1885), p. 97.

5 BAD PUBLIC RELATIONS

1 Christopher Smart, 'Jubilate Agno', Manuscript Eng 719, Houghton Library, Harvard University (1759–63).

2 Vincenz A. Kollar, *Treatise on Insects Injurious to Gardeners, Foresters, and Farmers* (London, 1840), p. 33.

3   Charles Gardiner, 'The Old Cotswold Dialect: Birds, Beasts and
    Flowers', *Evesham Journal*, (12 February 1960).
4   Thomas Muffet, *The Theatre of Insects; or, Lesser Living Creatures as
    Bees, Flies, Caterpillars, Spiders, Worms, and Co., a Most Elaborate
    Work* (London, 1658), p. 928.
5   Edward Step, *Bees, Wasps, Ants and Allied Insects of the British Isles*
    (London, 1932), pp. 34–5.
6   Alex Smith, *Ella the Ladybird* (London, 2018).
7   Charles Dickens, *The Uncommercial Traveller* (London, 1860).
8   Robert E. Wagner and D. A. Reierson, 'Yellow Jacket Control
    by Baiting. 1. Influence of Toxicants and Attractants on Bait
    Acceptance', *Journal of Economic Entomology*, 62 (1969),
    pp. 1192–7.
9   Ian C. Beavis, *Insects and Other Invertebrates in Classical Antiquity*
    (Exeter, 1988), p. 194.
10 Edward V. Lucas, ed., *The Works of Charles and Mary Lamb*
    (London, 1903).
11 Jonathon Jones, 'The Top 10 Picnics in Art', www.theguardian.com
    (21 August 2014).
12 George Orwell, 'Notes on the Way', *Time and Tide* (30 March–
    6 April 1940).
13 Iain Banks, *The Wasp Factory* (London, 1984).
14 Barrett A. Klein, 'The Curious Connection between Insects and
    Dreams', *Insects*, 3 (2012), pp. 1–17.
15 Seiran Sumner and G. Law, 'Why We Love Bees and Hate Wasps',
    Ecological Entomology, 43 (2018), pp. 836–45.

6 TABLOID MAYHEM

1   James H. Barnard, 'Studies of 400 Hymenoptera Sting Deaths in
    the United States', *Journal of Allergy and Clinical Immunology*, 52
    (1973), pp. 259–64.
2   J. W. Krombach et al., 'Pharaoh Menes' Death after an Anaphylactic
    Reaction – the End of a Myth', *Allergy: European Journal of Allergy
    and Clinical Immunology*, 59 (2004), pp. 1234–5.

3   Vincenz A. Kollar, *Treatise on Insects Injurious to Gardeners, Foresters, and Farmers* (London, 1840), p. 34.

4   Richard S. H. Pumphrey, 'Fatal Anaphylaxis in the UK, 1992–2001', in *Anaphylaxis: Novartis Foundation Symposium 257*, ed. G. Bock and J. Goode (2008), pp. 116–28.

5   Steven J. Falk, '*Dolichovespula media* (Retzius): A New British Social Wasp', *Proceedings and Transactions of the British Entomological Society*, 15 (1982), pp. 14–16.

6   George W. Allen and Michael E. Archer, '*Dolichovespula saxonica* (Fabricius, 1793) (Hym., Vespidae) Found in Britain, with a Key to British *Dolichovespula*', *Entomologist's Monthly Magazine*, 125 (1989), pp. 103–5.

7   Anthony Fitzherbert, *Boke of Husbandrie* (London, 1534).

8   Alfred Tennyson, *The Princess: A Medley* (London, 1847).

9   Richard J. Harris, 'Diet of the Wasps *Vespula vulgaris* and *V. germanica* in Honeydew Beech Forest of the South Island, New Zealand', *New Zealand Journal of Zoology*, 18 (1991), pp. 159–69.

10 Andrew Alderson, 'This Painting is "Expulsion and Killing of an Enemy". What Does it Tell Us about Gordon Brown?', www.thetelegraph.co.uk (13 August 2006).

11 Richard Kearton, *Wild Nature's Ways* (London, 1909), p. 140.

12 Quoted by J. Philip Spradbery in *Wasps* (London, 1973), p. 286.

13 Jacob Ishay, Bytinski H. Salz and A. Shulov, 'Contributions to the Bionomics of the Oriental Hornet (*Vespa orientalis* Fab.)', *Israel Journal of Entomology*, 2 (1967), pp. 45–106.

14 John Lubbock, *Ants, Bees and Wasps: A Record of Observations on the Habits of the Social Hymenoptera* (London, 1882).

15 John H. Comstock, *An Introduction to Entomology* (Ithaca, 1947), p. 977.

16 Edward Step, *Insect Artizans and their Work* (London, 1919).

17 William S. Dallas, *Elements of Entomology: An Outline of the Natural History and Classification of British Insects* (London, 1857), p. 270.

18 J. G. Wood, *Homes Without Hands: Being a Description of the Habitations of Animals, Classed According to their Principle of Construction* (London, 1866), p. 139.

19 J. G. Wood, *Nature's Teachings: Human Invention Anticipated by Nature* (London, 1907), pp. 166–8.

20 Arabella Buckley, *Life and Her Children: Glimpses of Animal Life from the Amoeba to the Insects* (London, 1880), pp. 267–8.

21 Arthur Mee, ed., *The Children's Encyclopedia* (London, *c*. 1950), p. 5841.

22 Ibid., p. 1294.

23 Jacob C. Schäffer, *Versuche und Muster, ohne alle Lumpen oder doch mit einem geringen Zusatze derselben, Papier zu machen* (Regensburg, 1765).

24 John A. Smart, *Handbook for the Identification of Insects of Medical Importance* (London, 1943), p. 201.

7 WHAT IS THE POINT OF WASPS?

1   Dylan Thomas, *A Child's Christmas in Wales* (London, 1955).

2   Edmund Sanders, *A Beast Book for the Pocket: The Vertebrates of Britain, Wild and Domestic, Other than Birds and Fishes* (Oxford, 1937), p. 152.

3   Edward Topsell, *History of Four-footed Beasts and Serpents* (London, 1658), p. 657.

4   Ibid., p. 660.

5   Robin Edwards, ed., *Social Wasps: Their Biology and Control* (East Grinstead, 1980), pp. 130–45.

6   Michael E. Archer, 'The Weights of Forager Loads of *Paravespula vulgaris* (Linn.) (Hymenoptera: Vespidae) and the Relationship of Load Weight to Forager Size', *Insects Sociaux*, 24 (1977), pp. 95–102.

7   Jacob Ishay, Bytinski H. Salz and A. Shulov, 'Contributions to the Bionomics of the Oriental Hornet (*Vespa orientalis* Fab.)', *Israel Journal of Entomology*, 2 (1967), pp. 45–106.

8   Richard J. Harris and E. H. Oliver, 'Prey Diets and Populations Densities of the Wasps *Vespula vulgaris* and *V. germanica* in Scrubland-pasture', *New Zealand Journal of Ecology*, 17 (1993), pp. 5–12.

9   Edward Latham Ormerod, *British Social Wasps: An Introduction to their Anatomy and Physiology, Architecture, and General Natural*

History, with Illustrations of their Different Species and their Nests (London, 1868).

10 Henry A. Ballou, 'Report on the Prevalence of Some Pests and Diseases in the West Indies during 1912', *Barbados West Indies Bulletin*, 13 (1913), pp. 333–57.

11 Howard E. Evans and Mary J. W. Eberhard, *The Wasps* (Newton Abbot, 1973).

12 Richard A. Jones, '*Vespula germanica* (F.) Wasps Hunting Dung Beetles *Aphodius contaminatus* (L.)', *Proceedings and Transactions of the British Entomological and Natural History Society*, 17 (1984), pp. 36–7.

13 Mick O'Hare, ed., *Does Anything Eat Wasps? And 101 Other Questions* (London, 2005).

14 Topsell, *History*, p. 655.

15 Christian Rossetti, *The Goblin Market and Other Poems* (London, 1862), lines 415–17.

16 Miguel Moreno and Ernest Giralt, 'Three Valuable Peptides from Bee and Wasp Venoms for Therapeutic and Biotechnological Use: Melittin, Apamin and Mastoparan', *Toxins (Basel)*, 7 (2015), pp. 1126–50.

17 Natalia B. Leite et al., 'PE and PS Lipids Synergistically Enhance Membrane Poration by a Peptide with Anticancer Properties', *Biophysical Journal*, 109 (2015), pp. 936–47.

18 Juliana Silva et al., 'Pharmacological Alternatives for the Treatment of Neurodegenerative Disorders: Wasp and Bee Venoms and their Components as New Neuroactive Tools', *Toxins*, 7 (2015), pp. 3179–209.

19 Topsell, *History*, p. 656.

20 Danielle O. Kisluk-Grosheide, Wolfram Koeppe and W. William Rider, *European Furniture in the Metropolitan Museum of Art: Highlights of the Collection* (New York, 2006), p. 28.

21 James Parker, *A Glossary of Terms used in Heraldry* (Oxford, 1847).

1   Jacob Meydenback (publisher), *Hortus Sanitatis* (Mainz, 1491).

2   Thomas Muffet, *The Theatre of Insects; or, Lesser Living Creatures as Bees, Flies, Caterpillars, Spiders, Worms, and Co., a Most Elaborate Work* (London, 1658).

3   Robert Hooke, *Micrographia; or, Some Physiological Descriptions of Minute Bodies made by Magnifying Glasses, with Observations and Inquiries Thereupon* (London, 1665).

4   Jan Swammerdam, *The Book of Nature; or, The History of Insects: Reduced to Distinct Classes, Confirmed by Particular Instances, Displayed in the Anatomical Analysis of Many Species . . . etc.* (London, 1758).

5   Ibid., p. 197.

6   Matthew Cobb, 'Jan Swammerdam on Social Insects: A View from the Seventeenth Century', *Insects Sociaux*, 49 (2002), pp. 92–7.

7   René A. F. de Réaumur, 'Histoire des Guespes', *Mémoires de l'Academie Royale des Sciences, Paris*, 19 (1719), pp. 302–64.

8   Carolus Linnaeus, *Systema Naturae per Regna Tria Naturae, Secundum Classes, Ordines, Genera, Species cum Characteribus Differentiis, Synonymis, Locis* (Holmiae, 1758).

9   Carl G. Thomson, 'Ofversigt af Sveriges Vesparuae', *Opuscula Entomologica*, 1 (1869), pp. 78–82.

10 Sievert A. Rohwer, 'The Hymenoptera, or Wasp-like Insects of Connecticut', *Guide to the Insects of Connecticut*, part 3: *Connecticut Geological and Natural History Survey Bulletin*, 22 (1916), pp. 640–43.

11 Henri de Saussure, *Études sur la Famile des Vespides*, vol. II: *Monographie des Guêpes Sociales* (Paris, 1853–8).

12 Edward Latham Ormerod, *British Social Wasps: An Introduction to their Anatomy and Physiology, Architecture, and General Natural History, with Illustrations of their Different Species and their Nests* (London, 1868).

13 Ibid., pp. 194–5.

14 Ibid., pp. 253–4.

15   Eleanor Anne Ormerod, *A Manual of Injurious Insects with Methods of Prevention and Remedy for their Attacks to Food Crops, Forest Trees and Fruit: to which is Appended a Short Introduction to Entomology* (London, 1890); Eleanor Anne Ormerod, *Handbook of Insects Injurious to Orchard and Bush Fruits with Means of Prevention and Remedy* (London, 1898).

16   Caspar A. Hallmann et al., 'More than 75 Percent Decline in Total Flying Insect Biomass in Protected Areas', *Plos One*, https://doi. org (19 October, 2017).

17   Michael E. Archer, 'Current Knowledge of British Aculeate Hymenoptera with Special Reference to the Occurrence of High Quality Species in Priority Habitats', *British Journal of Entomology and Natural History*, 20 (2007), pp. 75–94.

18   Michael E. Archer, '*Vespa crabro* Linnaeus, 1759', in *Provisional Atlas of the Aculeate Hymenoptera of Britain and Ireland, Part 1*, ed. Robin Edwards (Abbots Ripton, 1997), pp. 56–7.

Select Bibliography

Ainsworth Davis, James R., *The Natural History of Animals*
(London, 1905)

Badenoch, L. N., *Romance of the Insect World* (London, 1893)

Beavis, Ian C., *Insects and Other Invertebrates in Classical Antiquity*
(Exeter, 1988)

Brooks, Richard, *The Natural History of Insects with their Properties
and Uses in Medicine* (London, 1763)

Budgen, L. M., *Episodes of Insect Life* (London, 1850)

Cloudsley-Thompson, John L., *Insects and History* (London, 1976)

Donovan, Edward, *The Natural History of British Insects: Explaining
them in their Several States, with the Periods of their Transformations,
their Food, Oeconomy etc*. (London, 1792–1813)

Edwards, Robin, *Social Wasps: Their Biology and Control*
(East Grinstead, 1980)

Evans, Howard E., and Mary J. W. Eberhard, *The Wasps*
(Newton Abbot, 1973)

Fabre, Jean-Henri, *Fabre's Book of Insects*, retold by Mrs Rodolph
Stawall, illustrated by E. J. Detmold (New York, 1921)

Gauld, Ian, and Barry Bolton, eds, *The Hymenoptera*
(Oxford, 1989)

Kollar, Vincenz A., *Treatise on Insects Injurious to Gardeners, Foresters,
and Farmers* (London, 1840)

Lubbock, John, *Ants, Bees and Wasps: A Record of Observations on
the Habits of the Social Hymenoptera* (London, 1882)

Michelet, Jules, *The Insect* (London, 1875)

Muffet, Thomas, *The Theatre of Insects; or, Lesser Living Creatures as Bees, Flies, Caterpillars, Spiders, Worms, and Co., a Most Elaborate Work* (London, 1658)

Ormerod, Edward Latham, *British Social Wasps: An Introduction to their Anatomy and Physiology, Architecture, and General Natural History, With Illustrations of their Different Species and their Nests* (London, 1868)

Packard, Alpheus S., *A Text-Book of Entomology, Including the Anatomy, Physiology, Embryology and Metamorphoses of Insects* (New York, 1898)

Saunders, Edward, *Hymenoptera Aculeata of the British Isles* (London, 1896)

Schmidt, Justin O., *The Sting of the Wild* (Baltimore, MD, 2016)

Shaw, George, *General Zoology or Systematic Natural History* (London, 1806)

Spradbery, J. Philip, *Wasps* (London, 1973)

Step, Edward, *Marvels of Insect Life: A Popular Account of Structure and Habitat* (London, 1915)

—, *Bees, Wasps, Ants and Allied Insects of the British Isles* (London, 1932)

Swammerdam, Jan, *The Book of Nature; or, the History of Insects: Reduced to Distinct Classes, Confirmed by Particular Instances, Displayed in the Anatomical Analysis of Many Species . . . etc.* (London, 1758)

Topsell, Edward, *History of Four-footed Beasts and Serpents* (London, 1658)

Wood, J. G., *Homes Without Hands: Being a Description of the Habitations of Animals, Classed According to their Principle of Construction* (London, 1866)

—, *Nature's Teachings: Human Invention Anticipated by Nature* (London, 1907)

Associations and Websites

ANAPHYLAXIS CAMPAIGN
www.anaphylaxis.org.uk
Information and support for anaphylaxis sufferers

BEES, WASPS AND ANTS RECORDING SOCIETY
www.bwars.com
Information on British aculeate Hymenoptera

BIG WASP SURVEY
www.bigwaspsurvey.org
Citizen science project to monitor social wasps in the UK

BRITISH PEST CONTROL ASSOCIATION
https://bpca.org.uk
Trade association for pest control companies in Britain

FLICKR
www.flickr.com/photos/63075200@N07/
collections/72157629294465012
Entomologist Steven Falk's photo guide to UK social wasps

NHS CHOICES
www.nhs.uk/conditions/insect-bites-and-stings
Medical help and advice relating to insect bites and stings

NON-NATIVE SPECIES SECRETARIAT
www.nonnativespecies.org
Check the alerts link for up-to-date information on the Asian hornet,
Vespa velutina

NOTTINGHAMSHIRE INVERTEBRATE FAUNA
www.eakringbirds.com/eakringbirds2/insectswaspsidentification.htm
Excellent photo identification guide to social wasp species

Acknowledgements

I got my interest in natural history from my late father, Alfred Jones, and because of him I grew up never being scared of wasps, knowing that the males could not sting anyway, and with a fair understanding of why there were worker females as well as a queen in the nest. Even as a young teenager I remember at least one of my school chums asking that age-old question: 'And what is the point of wasps?' I hope this book, long in the coming, is some answer.

Verity Ure-Jones was my first arbiter and critic, reading through the entire draft text during her daily commutes, and pointing out where I had repeated myself, or where I had not explained something very clearly. Lillian Ure-Jones took up the baton near the end of the process and helped with the proof-reading.

Elsewhere along the way many people have given help and made useful suggestions, including: John Barrett, Vanna Bartlett, Laura Bax, Matthew Cobb, Laurence Beale Collins, Stephen Boulton, Tony Canning, Allison Carpenter, Susannah English, Ema Felix, Adam Glasser, Sarah Gould, Karen Hanley, David Hibling, Greg Hitchcock, David Hooper, Caroline Jones, Catherine Jones, Rob King, Hilary Marchant, Ian Marchant, Chris McGaw, Chris Merry, Penny Metal, Kate Morgan, Nicky Morgan, John Norton, Anne Phillips, Jo Priestnall, Ian Quance, Betty Rees, Janette Renshaw, Stuart Roberts, Jony Russell, Helen Sargan, Michael Schwaabe, Laura Shreeve, Carly Silver, Claudia Watts, Brett Westwood, Ian Whiteley and Paul Williams.

Finally, thank you again Catrina Ure for love and support for all the usual things bug.

Photo Acknowledgements

The author and the publishers wish to express their thanks to the below sources of illustrative material and/or permission to reproduce it.

Ainsworth Davis, *The Natural History of Animals*, photo courtesy of the author: p. 86; Badenoch, *Romance of the Insect World*, photo courtesy of the author: p. 81; Bewick, *A General History of Quadrupeds*, photo courtesy of the author: p. 102; Brooks, *The Natural History of Insects*, photo courtesy of the author: pp. 82, 90; Detmold, *Fabre's Book of Insects*, photo courtesy of the author: p. 110; Donovan, *The Natural History of British Insects*, photo courtesy of the author: p. 10; DSIR New Zealand: p. 94; *Episodes of Insect Life*, photo courtesy of the author: pp. 8, 73; The J. Paul Getty Museum: p. 38; *Hortus sanitatis*, University of Cambridge Digital Library: p. 45 left and right; Hogg, *The Microscope*, photo courtesy of the author: p. 22; Richard Jones photos: pp. 6, 13, 24, 31, 43 left and right, 51 top, 74, 79 bottom, 84, 85, 89, 92, 100, 112, 123, 125, 147, 149, 150, 153, 157, 159, 174; Richard Jones, ephemera in author's collection: pp. 28, 42, 57, 71, 108, 118, 124, 126, 152; Library of Congress, Washington, DC: pp. 109, 158; Los Angeles County Museum of Art (LACMA): p. 57 bottom right; Lydekker, *The Royal Natural History*: p. 175; Penny Metal: pp. 67, 83, 168, 176, 177; The Metropolitan Museum of Art, New York: pp. 52, 53 top and bottom; Michlet, *The Insect*, photo courtesy of the author: pp. 172, 178; Muffet, *Theatre of Insects*, Biodiversity Heritage Library: p: 162, 165; National Audubon Society: p. 78; Ormerod, *Wasps*, photo courtesy of the author: p. 104, 105; Packard, *Text Book of Entomology*,

Index

Page numbers in *italics* refer to illustrations